Classroom Assessment Techniques

A Handbook for Faculty

K. Patricia Cross
and
Thomas A. Angelo

Prepared for the National Center for Research
to Improve Postsecondary Teaching and Learning

The project presented, or reported herein, was performed pursuant to a grant from the Office of Educational Research and Improvement/Department of Education (OERI/ED). However, the opinions expressed herein do not necessarily reflect the position or policy of the OERI/ED and no official endorsement by the OERI/ED should be inferred.

Classroom Assessment Techniques

A Handbook for Faculty

CONTENTS

ACKNOWLEDGEMENTS

In preparing a handbook of this type, our debt to others is especially great. First, we are building on the ideas, research, and experiences of many scholars and practitioners who have sought ways to improve the educational experiences of undergraduate students.

We have drawn especially heavily on the work of Benjamin Bloom and his colleagues, who, in the 1950s and 1960s, laid the groundwork for the classification and measurement of educational objectives. This same group of scholars and researchers also developed methods for "formative evaluation" which, as the name implies, emphasizes conducting assessments while the processes of teaching and learning are fluid and susceptible to modification.

We are also indebted to those scholars and researchers who engaged in the prodigious work of synthesizing the vast research literature concerning the impact of college on students. Were it not for those who stop occasionally to take stock of what we know about the effects of education on students, we would be inundated by research and publications that fly off in all directions, without moving our collective knowledge of teaching and learning forward. Among those to whom we are indebted for the syntheses that underlie much of our work are: Alexander Astin, Howard Bowen, Arthur Chickering, Kenneth Feldman, Theodore Newcomb, and C. Robert Pace.

On a more current note, we express our gratitude to the authors of the excellent literature reviews that constitute the fruits of the first year's labor of NCRIPTAL (National Center for Research to Improve Postsecondary Teaching and Learning, University of Michigan). The syntheses produced by Harold Korn (1986), and by Wilbert McKeachie, Paul Pintrich, Yi-Guang Lin, and David Smith (1986) were especially useful to us in preparing this handbook.

We are also grateful to three organizations that provided resources, support, and staff time to prepare this handbook. NCRIPTAL provided summer support for the work of K. Patricia Cross in reviewing the literature and developing the concept of classroom research. The Harvard Seminar on Assessment provided support for Thomas A. Angelo in searching the literature and developing, adapting, and categorizing assessment techniques. The Harvard Graduate School of Education provided essential secretarial and staff support for the preparation of this handbook. Three of the school's staff members, Mary Sullivan, Norma Diala, and Jane Gerloff, deserve our special thanks for their help throughout the project.

In the best spirit of academic cooperation, these three organizations—NCRIPTAL, the Harvard Seminar on Assessment, and Harvard's Graduate School of Education—joined in supporting the search for ways to improve the self-assessment of college teaching. We express our sincere appreciation to all of them.

K. Patricia Cross and Thomas A. Angelo   January 1988
                                                    Cambridge, Massachusetts

INTRODUCTION

This handbook is part of a larger effort to improve teaching and learning in traditional college classrooms. We believe that classroom teachers can, through close observation, the collection of feedback on student learning, and the design of experiments, learn more about how students learn, and more specifically, how students respond to particular teaching approaches. We call this process of involving teachers in the formal study of teaching and learning *Classroom Research*.

Our model of Classroom Research is based on five assumptions. They are stated below, along with some brief observations about their applicability to the present scene in education.

Assumption One

The quality of student learning is directly—although not exclusively—related to the quality of classroom teaching. Therefore, the first and most promising way to improve learning is to improve teaching.

The past five years have been a period of intense examination of education in the United States. Blue-ribbon commissions have been convened, reports have been written, recommendations made, and legislation proposed and passed—all in the interest of improving the quality of education. So far, the most common response to the demands for reform has been "assessment."

While collecting and analyzing information about student learning seems an appropriate place to start, we believe that present assessment efforts are taking place too far from the scene of the action. Most of the enthusiasm for assessment is generated at collegewide and statewide levels, primarily by administrators and legislators responding to public demand for accountability. The results have been large-scale institutional or system-level assessments, efforts that have too often devoted inadequate attention to creating the necessary linkages between assessing and improving instruction.

After statewide and institutional assessments have been completed, the critical question that remains to be answered is, *How can we improve student learning?* The answer to that question lies with the teaching faculty, and the purpose of Classroom Research is to involve classroom teachers from the very beginning in the formulation of goals and the collection of information about student learning.

Assumption Two

To improve their teaching, teachers need to make their goals and objectives explicit. They also need to receive specific, comprehensible feedback on the extent to which they are achieving those goals and objectives.

The two major products of our work on Classroom Research are the Teaching Goals Inventory (TGI) and this handbook of classroom assessment techniques for teachers.

The Teaching Goals Inventory is a 48-item questionnaire that helps teachers clarify and establish instructional priorities appropriate to their subject matter and their students. The TGI is currently in experimental stages, and our goal in continuing to refine it is to develop an instrument that will help teachers explicitly define their teaching goals so that they can then collect the types of feedback about student learning most relevant to assessing those goals.

Classroom assessment techniques is the name we give to instruments and methods designed to inform teachers *what* students are learning in the classroom and *how well* they are learning it. The assessment techniques described in this handbook represent a first attempt to provide suggestions to teachers on how to get concrete feedback about the level and quality of student learning.

As we prepared the descriptions of these assessment techniques, we discovered a healthy, dynamic tension between giving suggestions about teaching techniques to accomplish desired learning ends and giving suggestions about ways to find out whether goals are being accomplished. Are the techniques described herein "teaching tips" or "assessment techniques"?

They are both, and we believe that their dual nature is a strength. Each assessment technique has an implied teaching goal (stated under "Purpose" in the description), and it also provides information about how well that goal has been accomplished. It might be more appropriate to speak of "feedback loops"—from teaching technique to feedback on student learning to revision of the technique. This loop establishes, between assessment and instruction, the linkages so critical to improving the quality of undergraduate education.

Assumption Three

The research most likely to improve teaching and learning is that conducted by teachers on questions they themselves have formulated in response to problems or issues in their own teaching.

Teachers have been criticized for their failure to apply the findings of research to their teaching almost as often as researchers have been taken to task for failing to ask the research questions that are meaningful and useful to practitioners. For most of this century, the gap between research and practice has posed a major problem to those funding research in education. "Development" and "dissemination" have been the presumed answers, but the fact is that those two stalwarts of converting research in the laboratory into practice in the field have not worked as well in education as in agricultural extension, the model upon which "R & D" in education is based.

The goal of Classroom Research is to reduce the distance between researchers and practitioners to zero. It is our way of assuring that the questions investigated by the researcher are meaningful and useful to the practitioner. This should not imply that we think educational research is therefore useless. Quite the contrary, it is our conviction that as practitioners become involved in raising questions and conducting their own research on learning, they will be more interested in, more appreciative of, and better able to make use of the fundamental and generalized findings that are the special province of educational researchers.

Assumption Four

Inquiry and intellectual challenge are powerful sources of motivation, growth, and renewal for college teachers, and Classroom Research can provide such challenge.

In the September/October 1985 issue of *Change,* the editors discussed the poor morale and lack of professional identity widespread among college teachers in the 1980s. The proposed solutions were many, but one that worries us is the growing tendency to push faculty members toward greater identification with their academic disciplines through the singular path of research and publication in the discipline.

We question the implicit assumption that academic research and scholarly publication are the most appropriate routes to professional achievement for all faculty members and to academic excellence for all postsecondary institutions. The drive for "academic excellence" has all too often been confused with the drive to be more like Harvard or Stanford or the University of Michigan, where the mission of the institution is in part to push back the frontiers of knowledge through research. We believe that teachers need intellectual challenge, but we assert that it is to be found in many activities—through research, scholarly study, and the formal study of teaching and learning.

Most colleges and universities in this country are teaching institutions, and most faculty—70 percent according to the recent Carnegie survey (*Chronicle of Higher Education,* Dec. 18, 1985)—are more interested in teaching than in research. Why shouldn't faculty members be encouraged to achieve professional identity and intellectual challenge through doing research on and continuing to learn about that which enhances their ability to achieve high levels of competence in their chosen profession—teaching? Classroom Research is an effort to develop knowledgeable, involved, highly competent teachers.

Assumption Five

There is nothing so esoteric, mysterious, or fragile about Classroom Research that it cannot be entrusted to and done by anyone capable of and dedicated to college teaching.

The goals of Classroom Research differ from those of traditional educational research. Educational researchers need to be highly trained in sampling theory, in tests of significance, in the collection and management of frequently large pools of data, or in the increasingly specialized methods of qualitative research.

The classroom researcher, on the other hand, usually needs few of the specialized research methods required for generalizing findings. The purpose of the classroom researcher is *not* to discover the "general laws" of learning but to find out what specific students are learning as a result of a given teacher's efforts.

We believe that the more classroom teachers engage in Classroom Research, the more sophisticated and knowledgeable they will become about teaching and learning. It is our contention that Classroom Research is a fundamentally *different* science from educational research and that appropriate tools and methods can be competently designed and used by teachers who know the structure of their discipline and the characteristics of their students.

The purpose of this handbook, then, is to provide classroom teachers—from all sorts of disciplinary specialities and backgrounds—some entry-level tools for assessing the learning of their students.

Criteria for Selecting Classroom Assessment Techniques

The assessment techniques presented in this handbook have two basic sources. Some are culled from an extensive review of the literature of both secondary and postsecondary education. Others come from our own teaching repertoires. Regardless of their source, most of the feedback devices presented in this book were devised by classroom teachers rather than by measurement "experts." In their original forms, many of these assessment techniques were presented as "teaching tips." In such cases, we have redesigned and refocused them by augmenting how-to descriptions with our own comments on pros and cons, suggestions for most appropriate applications, and ideas on the analysis and interpretation of the data collected through their use.

The following questions guided our search for and selection of classroom assessment techniques:

1. Will the assessment technique provide information about what students are learning in individual classrooms?

2. Does the technique focus on "alterable variables"—aspects of teacher or learner behavior that can be changed to promote better learning?

3. Will it give teachers and students information they can use to make midcourse changes and corrections?

4. Is the assessment technique relatively simple to prepare and use?

5. Are the results from the use of the technique relatively quick and easy to analyze?

A positive answer to all five questions meant the technique was probably appropriate to our needs. In assembling this collection of classroom assessment techniques, we aimed for broad coverage, a variety of types, and a range of complexity. We looked for strategies that could provide quantitative or qualitative data, written or oral feedback, and information on individuals, small groups, or entire classes.

We also felt that these techniques should allow for and encourage varying degrees of teacher modification and innovation. As a consequence, these assessment techniques range from off-the-shelf, "ready made" devices designed for immediate application, to "do-it-yourself" designs, that present ideas for teachers to adapt and develop.

To our knowledge, this is the first serious effort to meld "assessment techniques" with "teaching tips." There are books on how to measure learning, and there are books on teaching methods. They arise from two separate streams of expertise in education, and no one has systematically tried to develop the syntheses that would result in assessment techniques that teach and teaching methods that assess learning. To be sure, testing experts have talked occasionally about the desirability of using the "psychology" of the testing moment to teach, and a few of those writing about teaching methods have encouraged teachers to observe carefully, if not systematically, the response of learners to teaching, but by and large the two streams of expertise have run their separate courses.

Having worked hard at this synthesis, we now offer the *Handbook* as a "first cut," with the expectation that these concrete examples of assessment/teaching techniques will stimulate other teachers both to improve these techniques and to develop and share their own.

Developing this handbook also involved a second type of synthesis—one that has a checkered history in the literature of education—the synthesis of content and process. Ideally a teacher must know *what* to teach as well as *how* to teach. While almost everyone acknowledges the importance of both content and process, pedagogy in different periods of history emphasizes one over the other, and the preparation of teachers may vary greatly depending on level and philosophy of those in charge of the preparation. There is a reaction now against what many perceive as an overemphasis on process; that is, on "teaching methods," for teachers in public schools. And there is an equal and opposite reaction to the lack of attention given to teaching and learning in the preparation of doctoral students for their futures as college teachers.

The terminology common in teacher education today speaks of "domain-specific" and "generic" teaching methods. There are some generic teaching methods appropriate in any field of study—those involving students actively in learning, for example. But good history teachers teach differently from good physics teachers, and those differences require domain-specific methods.

Our philosophy of Classroom Research *requires* the involvement of disciplinary specialists in the improvement of teaching and learning. We believe that expert history teachers have as much to contribute as education experts to the improvement of history teaching. We need the active participation of subject matter experts in designing and improving teaching/assessment techniques.

The problem for us came when we realized that, in this first cut at presenting concrete ideas, we would be limited to generic designs. Domain-specific assessment techniques will necessarily have to grow and develop through the participation of discipline-oriented faculty members in Classroom Research.

We do have, on the drawing board, plans for a computer network through which teachers in various disciplines, such as math teachers, can share domain-specific teaching/assessment techniques with math teachers across the country. Ultimately, our vision for Classroom Research depends on this participation and sharing among discipline-based faculty members.

We hope the generic examples included in this handbook will stimulate original designs, new techniques, and adaptations relevant to the enormous variety of teaching fields in higher education.

Organization of the Handbook

The body of this handbook is organized into three sections. Section I includes techniques for assessing academic skills and knowledge. Section II contains techniques for assessing students' self-awareness and self-assessment of learning skills. The techniques in Section III are designed to assess student reactions to teaching and courses.

The handbook begins with techniques to assess academic skills and knowledge. Helping students learn the subject matter of their courses is the most common goal of college teachers, and virtually all teachers try to get some indication of what students know about the subject being taught. But most teachers aspire to more than simply teaching students information about subject matter: they hope to use subject matter to teach students to think. They hope to teach them to solve problems, to analyze arguments, to synthesize information from different sources, and, in general, to help students develop higher-level cognitive skills.

From the 1950s through the 1970s, major advances were made in the description and measurement of "higher" cognitive outcomes, as Benjamin Bloom and other measurement specialists developed taxonomies of educational objectives (Bloom, 1956) and guidelines for formative and summative evaluation (Bloom, Hastings, & Madaus, 1971). In the last decade, educators and cognitive scientists have joined in attempts to promote the development of "creative" and "critical" thinking skills through direct instruction.

In organizing Section I, we have drawn on these streams of research and pedagogy. In the introduction to Section I, you will find a discussion of research on academic skills and intellectual development, with particular attention to the ways in which researchers and theorists conceptualize intellectual development. This is a period of great ferment in cognitive psychology, and there are multiple definitions of the proficiencies or abilities that constitute intellectual growth. These definitions are revealed in the variety of classification schemes presented in the introduction to Section I.

Section II presents a set of skills that have been the focus of attention recently. Cognitive psychologists call such skills *metacognitive* to convey the importance of students' attention to and awareness of their own learning processes.

Research shows that good students plan their learning, monitor it "in process," and assess their own skills as learners. Poor students, in contrast, are more likely to view learning as a set of facts and answers that are "out there" apart from themselves and their interaction with the subject matter.

Section II comprises two subsections. The first subsection presents some ideas for assessing students' capacity to observe themselves in the process of learning. This subsection also calls attention to the importance of promoting self-awareness and of providing students with opportunities for developing metacognitive skills. The second subsection suggests some ways to help students develop the ability to make accurate diagnoses of their learning skills. These devices also give teachers some insight into their students' self-assessment skills.

Section III contains assessment techniques most directly associated with information on teaching performance. In this section, we ask not so much *what* students are learning as *how* they perceive and react to the classroom experience and how they assess their own learning.

Recent research on the evaluation of teaching and learning suggests that students are both valid and reliable sources of information about teaching and how it affects them. Many teachers, especially beginning teachers, will find the direct access to student responses provided by these devices the most helpful information of all.

Section III is also based on the extensive and still developing literature of research and practice. At present, good syntheses of the state of the art in assessing student reactions to their classroom experiences are found largely in articles rather than in books. Among the most informative studies are those by Centra (1977a, 1977b), Feldman (1977), Gleason (1986), Kulik and McKeachie (1975), and Seldin (1984).

Although most of the work on teacher evaluation combines students' reactions to methods and materials into what is usually considered a comprehensive evaluation of the course, we found it useful to separate the two subsections.

The first subsection presents some suggestions that teachers might use to gauge the reactions of students to the teacher and his or her teaching methods. Students' responses to teachers and teaching methods are varied and frequently hidden from the teacher. Students' reactions range all the way from adopting the teacher as a personal model to emulate, to annoyance with small mannerisms, to feelings of frustration that the teaching is counterproductive to learning. Some of the assessment techniques described are open-ended, permitting students to reveal hitherto unsuspected reactions, while other techniques permit the teacher to investigate specific issues.

The second subsection concerns students' reactions to the materials, assignments, and activities of the course. These techniques direct attention more to a response to the course than to the teacher. While the separation into two subsections may seem somewhat arbitrary, we found that we could devise appropriate techniques for each subsection and concluded that teachers might also find the distinction helpful.

The overview to Section III contains a brief review of what we have learned from research on students' ability to critique teaching skills, course materials, activities, and assignments. To date, students have been used largely as evaluators of courses and teaching to help administrators make decisions about promotions and tenure. However, the assessment techniques presented in Section III are not for that purpose, rather they are designed to help teachers and students make decisions about which methods and materials are most helpful in promoting learning in the classroom.

Sections I, II, and III represent broad-stroke, topic-centered classifications. The subsections within each of these three sections represent functional clusterings of the assessment techniques. Within each subsection, we have organized the assessment techniques by their ratings on a rough, five-point, ease-of-use scale ranging from simple (I) to complex (V).

One problem with this unidimensional ease-of-use scale is that, quite frequently, devices that are easy to devise and administer are complex to score and interpret. This trade-off between front-end and back-end time commitments is, however, a familiar one to most classroom teachers. An essay exam, for example, usually requires quite a bit of time to read and interpret—a heavy back-end time commitment—but rather less time to develop. An effective multiple-choice test, on the other hand, is just the opposite. It requires a great deal of time to plan and produce—a heavy front-end commitment—but little time to score. The choice between these two familiar assessment techniques is often made on pragmatic considerations, such as the size of the class and the nature of the subject matter.

Our five-point classification probably leans more toward ease of administration than to ease of interpretation. This reflects the design of these techniques, a design that encourages teachers to decide on the depth and complexity of analysis and interpretation appropriate to their needs and interests. Our goal has been to offer a range of options so teachers can find the levels and types of techniques that suit their subject matter, students, teaching-style preferences, and the amount of time and energy they wish to devote to the assessment. We hope this range of choices encourages you to select the most "appropriate technology" for carrying out your own Classroom Research projects.

One of our early experiences in this project convinced us of the importance of providing options in assessment techniques. In the first administration of the Teaching Goals Inventory (TGI), we found that every single item of the 48 instructional goals included in the TGI received the full range of responses. For example, a goal that some teachers rated "essential" was rated "irrelevant" by others among their colleagues at the same institution (Cross & Fideler, in press).

If teaching goals differ, so too must the devices teachers use to measure whether goals have been achieved.

Based on our experience with the enormous variation in teaching goals, we expect that some teachers will find certain of the techniques included here useful and helpful while others will reject them as inappropriate and irrelevant. Our hope is that each teacher will find one or more assessment techniques that can be used as presented—or better yet, that can be adapted or modified to fit the precise requirements of that teacher.

Five Guidelines for Successfully Using Assessment Techniques

Guideline 1:   Don't try any technique in this book that doesn't appeal to your intuition and your experienced judgment as a teacher.

The first and most important guideline is to remember that all of the techniques presented in this handbook *are meant to be suggestions* and should be taken as such. We believe that individual classroom teachers are the best authorities about what is and is not likely to help them improve their own teaching.

Guideline 2:   Don't make self-assessment into a self-inflicted chore or burden.

This second major suggestion stems from our faith in ongoing, incremental improvement. We believe that it's ultimately more effective and satisfying to try out *one* of these techniques in a semester—and fully and calmly work it through— than to try out *three* only to become overwhelmed and discouraged.

Guideline 3:   Do choose techniques that seem likely to provide assessment information that will benefit both you and your students in tangible ways and that will serve as learning exercises—even if they ultimately fail as assessment techniques.

This suggestion aims at ensuring that both your students and you get some worthwhile return on your investments of time and energy, whether or not the assessment objectives of the techniques are fully realized. We believe that Classroom Research should, as much as possible, avoid the means/ends dichotomy that characterizes much institutional assessment. That is, techniques for assessing classroom learning ought to reflect, reinforce, and promote the same learning goals that they examine and document.

Guideline 4:   Don't ask your students to use any technique you haven't previously tried yourself.

In addition to being a reflection of our basic concern with fair play and belief in the Golden Rule, this suggestion is meant to help you avoid wasted time and effort as well as to ensure effective use of these techniques. By trying out the assessment techniques on yourself first, you can find out whether the techniques are really appropriate, where problems are likely to occur, whether any modifications are necessary, and how long it takes to go through them. In assessment, as in teaching, thoughtful preparation and rehearsal are major parts of successful performance.

Guideline 5:   Do take into account that administering an assessment technique and analyzing the feedback from it, particularly the first time, is likely to take at least twice as much time to complete as your original, best estimate allows.

General Comments on Analyzing the Data You Collect

Virtually all of the techniques presented in this handbook generate data that can be analyzed and assessed either quantitatively or qualitatively, or by a combination of the two approaches. Given the formative aims of Classroom Research, we are convinced that a combined approach is often the most enlightening and useful.

Before deciding *how* to analyze the information that has been collected through the use of assessment techniques, however, it is important to clarify *why* you are analyzing it. Your original purpose for assessing learning in your classroom—to assess your students' knowledge of subject matter or reactions to the course, for example—should determine how you analyze the data.

All quantitative data analysis is based on counting, categorizing, and comparing numbers and proportions of items. At the simplest level, we use quantitative analyses to answer the questions how much or how many. A quantitative analysis of student responses to classroom assessment techniques can be as simple as counting the total number of items, or number of relevant items, listed or mentioned. One easy way to assess such lists is "vote counting," tallying the number of responses on the students' lists that match those on a master list. This is basically what happens when teachers score multiple-choice tests.

Qualitative analysis, on the other hand, provides answers to questions such as what kind, how well, and in what ways. To explain qualitative data analysis, we depend on narrating, explaining, and giving examples. A simple and familiar example of qualitative analysis often occurs when teachers read and evaluate essay exams or term papers.

The *skills* required to analyze data collected through classroom assessment techniques are familiar to most teachers and, as noted above, can be as simple as those used to evaluate and score tests and term papers. However, the *task* of analyzing data for Classroom Research differs in three important ways from the normal evaluation of student learning that takes place in classrooms. These differences concern purpose, unit of analysis, and the criteria on which the analysis is based.

When teachers analyze and assess tests and major assignments, they often have multiple and sometimes even conflicting purposes. One purpose is usually to give the students feedback on how much and how well they are learning. At the same time, teachers almost always have to grade the students' work for administrative purposes. The extrinsic, institutional demand for grades is often the most powerful motivator for the evaluation of student learning.

The data collected through use of classroom assessment techniques, to the contrary, should not be analyzed for grading purposes. The motivation for analyzing data collected through Classroom Research is intrinsic and personal in nature: it's driven by the teacher's desire to learn more about student learning in order to improve teaching.

The second major difference concerns the unit of analysis. In traditional classroom evaluations of student work, the primary unit of analysis is the individual student. It is the individual student's work that is evaluated, rated, ranked, and graded, even if class averages are computed and students are graded on the curve.

Classroom Research, on the other hand, focuses on the whole class, or groups within the class, as the primary unit of analysis. While results of this aggregate analysis may subsequently lead the teacher to focus on individual students, that is not its principal function. Classroom assessment techniques are aimed at collecting data on the class as a learning community.

The third difference concerns the type of criteria used and the explicitness with which teachers must define the criteria used in their analyses. In traditional classroom evaluation, the criteria for assessing student work are intimately linked to grading. Such criteria are often binary—right or wrong, acceptable or not, pass or fail. At other times, they may be scalar, as represented by the letter grades A through F, or the numbers 1 through 100. In either case, the criteria may be linked to an external standard, such as a national norm, or an internal standard, such as the class average. All such criteria are useful insofar as they make it possible to indicate, with one letter or number, the level of performance that the student has demonstrated. As such, they are primarily criteria for rating the products or outcomes of learning.

In teacher-directed Classroom Research, the criteria used in analyzing the students' responses depend greatly on the individual teacher's purpose for assessing and very little on institutional needs. The teacher is responsible for choosing or developing criteria to fit that purpose. We suspect that many teachers find it easier to judge an answer right or wrong than to analyze and assess a written record of the process that led to the answer. Nonetheless, the most useful criteria in classroom research are very often those which can be used to analyze processes and intermediate outcomes of learning—rather than the final products.

Perhaps the simplest way to sum up the difference between classroom evaluation used to grade individual students and classroom assessment techniques is to note that the primary purpose of the former is to classify, while that of the latter is to understand and change.

Suggestions for Analyzing the Data You Collect

What specific kinds of analysis do teachers need to transform raw data into information that will help them make instructional decisions? One way to begin to answer that question is to consider several possible general questions about student learning that teachers might want to answer through classroom assessment:

1. Questions about students

    a. How many students are learning well and how many aren't?
    b. Which students are learning well and which aren't?
    c. What do successful learners do that other learners don't do or don't do as well?

2. Questions about course content

    a. How much of the course content are students learning?
    b. Which elements of the course content are students learning?
    c. How well are students learning the course content?

3. Questions about teaching

    a. How does my teaching affect student learning, both positively and negatively?
    b. What specifically should I change about my teaching to promote optimal learning?
    c. How should I change those specific elements of my teaching to produce the greatest positive effects on learning?

General Suggestions for Using This Handbook

This is *not* a book to be read from cover to cover. It's a handbook, a reference book meant to be thumbed through for ideas and inspirations. We hope that teachers will consult it, mark it up, dog-ear the pages, add to it, revise it, and generally improve it as questions occur over the semester—or over the years—in the practice of teaching. To encourage this, there is space for notes following each technique. This is a book for teachers to make their own as they gain experience in the use of these assessment techniques and develop others.

To the best of our knowledge, many, if not most, of these ideas have had relatively limited exposure—even though some have appeared in print. Moreover, as noted earlier in this introduction, many of the techniques that *have* been published were intended and presented as teaching, not assessment, techniques. Third, there is little information available about teachers' experiences with self-assessment techniques—that is, there are very few assessments of the assessment techniques. Nonetheless, references are provided as a guide to further information about the assessment technique described.

While our literature search was extensive and thorough, we doubt that it was exhaustive. Therefore, we welcome any and all additions or corrections to the references. At the same time, we invite contributions to the collection of techniques presented herein, as well as comments on their effectiveness and suggestions for their adaptation and use.

In other words, we hope that teachers will not only use these techniques, but will assess their usefulness, improve on them, create new and better ones, and share their learning with us and with other teachers.

Techniques for Assessing Academic Skills and Intellectual Development

Overview

The goals of teachers differ, depending on their disciplines, the specific content of their courses, their students, and their own personal philosophies about the purposes of education. All teachers, however, are interested in the cognitive growth and academic skills of their students. In the drive toward academic excellence, the assessment of cognitive skills and mastery of subject matter has been given major attention, especially in institutional and statewide assessment plans. In terms of summative, large-scale evaluation, the assessment movement has had an important impact on the design and content of standardized tests and, to a lesser degree, of curricula and graduation requirements.

The impact of the assessment movement on the measurement of student learning in the classroom is less clear. Although classroom teachers have been testing students on their mastery of subject matter for centuries, there is growing conviction that classroom assessment resources are limited in scope and in usefulness. One problem is that traditional classroom tests are frequently used as summative evaluations—as "final" exams or other measures to grade students. They are not often used to provide feedback to both students and teachers on whether learning goals are being met.

Tests, however, are an effective way to define the goals of the course. Research suggests that students concentrate on learning whatever they think will be on the test. As McKeachie and his colleagues observe, "Whatever teachers' goals and no matter how clearly they present them, students' goals are strongly influenced by tests or the other activities that determine grades" (McKeachie, Pintrich, Lin, & Smith, 1986, p. 124). No matter how clear the teacher is about the "big picture," students are unlikely to share the view unless tests and other assessment measures point them toward it.

Formative, midcourse feedback at the classroom level, especially if it is repeated at regular intervals, helps both students and teachers clarify their goals and assess progress toward them. Furthermore, it does this while there is still time to make changes based on that feedback.

A second problem in current classroom assessments lies in the types of measures used. Many teacher-made measures concentrate on the lowest levels of intellectual skills, namely, on measuring students' abilities to remember and reproduce what is presented by others. Yet the emphasis in the 1980s reform movement is on the development of critical thinking, problem solving, and independent thought—the capacity to critically analyze the ideas of others and to generate ideas of one's own. This higher-order capacity is much more difficult to measure.

Assessing accomplishment in the cognitive domain has occupied educational psychologists for most of this century. "As yet, however, there is no comprehensive and universally accepted theory capturing complex human intellectual functions in a single conceptual framework" (Segal, Chipman, &

Glaser, 1985, p. 7). Research on the assessment of academic skills and intellectual development is in a period of especially rapid change right now, and a number of theories and taxonomies exist side by side.

The most influential mapping of the cognitive terrain for educational purposes is the extensive classification system devised by Bloom and his colleagues (Bloom, 1956; Bloom et al., 1971). The assumption underlying what has become known as the "Bloom Taxonomy" is that cognitive abilities can be measured along a continuum from simple to complex. A brief description of that taxonomy follows.

1.0	Knowledge	Recalling specific facts or general concepts. "Knowledge" as defined by Bloom et al., involves little more than bringing to mind the appropriate material.
2.0	Comprehension	Demonstrating the lowest level of understanding. The individual can make use of what is being communicated without necessarily relating it to other material or seeing its fullest implication.
3.0	Application	Using abstractions in concrete situations. The abstractions may be principles, ideas, and theories that must be remembered and applied.
4.0	Analysis	Breaking down a communication into its constituent elements. The relationships between ideas are made explicit and the organization of the communication is understood.
5.0	Synthesis	Putting together elements to form a whole. This involves arranging elements to constitute a structure not clearly there before.
6.0	Evaluation	Making judgments about the value of materials and methods for given purposes. The individual can make appraisals that satisfy criteria determined by the student or by others. (Bloom et al., 1971, pp. 271-273)

Another scheme that has been devised with a special eye to assessing college-student learning outcomes is one recommended by a recent study commission in New Jersey (Student Learning Outcomes Subcommittee, 1987). The New Jersey subcommittee is interested in measuring *general intellectual skills,* which they define as involving three proficiencies: The first set is labeled *getting information,* which involves the "process of internalizing and understanding the work of others: a book or a lecture, an argument or a theory, a work of art or a musical composition."

The second set of proficiencies has to do with *manipulating information.* This includes the Bloom categories of analysis—evaluating information presented by others—and synthesis—ordering, reordering, and synthesizing information provided by others.

The third set of proficiencies included in the New Jersey report involves *presenting information*—expressing one's own ideas intelligibly in oral, written, and graphic form.

Like the Bloom taxonomy, these categories can be translated into operational definitions, but the authors of the New Jersey report chose not to frame their definitions in a taxonomy or a theory. They note that while their proficiencies are "intimately interrelated; they are neither strictly sequential nor hierarchical; they are not neatly separable into mutually exclusive components" (p. 18).

A third classification of cognitive skills comes from a conference jointly sponsored by the National Institute of Education (NIE) and the Learning Research and Development Center (LRDC) of the University of Pittsburgh. That conference brought together cognitive researchers, program developers, and teachers of cognitive skills to discuss recent advances in thinking and learning. Two large volumes grew out of this conference. (See Segal, Chipman, & Glaser, 1985, Volume 1, and Chipman, Segal, & Glaser, 1985, Volume 2).

Their interest was in exploring the higher-level cognitive skills students need to understand, reason, solve problems, and learn. They devised three categories of such skills: knowledge acquisition, problem solving, and intelligence and reasoning.

Although the clustering is a bit different from both the Bloom taxonomy and the New Jersey definitions, the overall picture is quite similar. Under the category, *knowledge acquisition,* they include key cognitive skills such as "knowing when you know, knowing what you need to know, and knowing the utility of taking active steps to change your state of knowledge" (p. 7). In *problem solving,* the key learning skills include analyzing the problem, searching related knowledge, planning possible attempts at solution, keeping track of progress, and checking results against the overall goal or more immediate goals. Under *intelligence and reasoning,* they include such basic cognitive skills as approaching tasks in an organized, nonimpulsive fashion and drawing simple logical conclusions (Segal et al., 1985, p. 7).

Yet another view of the structure of cognition is presented by McKeachie and his colleagues (1986) at the National Center for Research to Improve Postsecondary Teaching and Learning (NCRIPTAL) at the University of Michigan. They conducted a comprehensive review of the literature on teaching and learning in higher education and decided to organize their discussion of student cognition under the rubrics of *knowledge structure, learning strategies,* and *thinking and problem solving.* Although these categories sound familiar, the emphasis of the NCRIPTAL group is less on *measuring* student outcomes than on *understanding* cognitive processes. For this reason, both their definitions and their measures are more complex than those of the Bloom and New Jersey schemes.

Under *knowledge structure,* they advocate study of both the structure of the subject matter and students' internal representations of that structure. Students' grasp of meaningful learning can be assessed, they say, by revealing or inferring the representation of the students' cognitive structure, indirectly by word association, card sorting, ordered-tree techniques, and interviews, and directly by concept mapping, networking, concept structuring and similar techniques (McKeachie et al., 1986, pp. 16-35).

Their second category of student cognition, *learning strategies,* deals with how students acquire and modify their knowledge base. McKeachie and his colleagues group these skills into three broad categories: cognitive, metacognitive, and resource management. "The cognitive category includes strategies related to the students' learning or encoding of material as well as strategies to facilitate retrieval of information. The metacognitive strategies involve strategies related to planning, regulating, monitoring, and modifying cognitive processes. The resource management strategies concern the students' strategies to control the resources (i.e., time, effort, outside support) that influence the quality and quantity of their involvement in the task" (McKeachie et al., 1986, p. 38).

The third category used by the NCRIPTAL investigators is *thinking and problem solving.* It includes critical thinking, problem solving, and reasoning—in general the use of learning in new situations to solve problems or make decisions. There has been a great deal of research on problem solving and critical thinking in recent years, and a number of instruments exist for the measurement of these skills (see McKeachie et al., 1986, pp. 58-68).

Today's excitement is in the recent advances made in the field of cognitive psychology. Both the Pittsburgh Center (LRDC) and the Michigan Center (NCRIPTAL) are investigating newer approaches to assimilative learning. The assimilative approach holds that meaningful learning occurs only when new inputs are linked with already existing schemata—that learning is a creative, active process, and that learners "create new knowledge out of what's already in their heads" (McKeachie et al., 1986).

Ausubel (1968), an early advocate of this school of cognition, writes that, "If I had to reduce all of educational psychology to just one principle, I would say this: `The most important single factor influencing learning is what the learner already knows. Ascertain this fact and teach him accordingly.'" If you accept this view of learning, then assessment depends not on tests, in the usual sense of questions asked and problems to be solved, but on the match between the conceptual map of the discipline or subject being taught and the internal cognitive map that illustrates what the learner knows.

It is not our intention to make classroom teachers into cognitive psychologists. Teachers have a responsibility and a desire to promote the intellectual development of their students, and some acquaintance with the developments in cognitive psychology is clearly desirable.

It is our contention, however, that classroom teachers, who understand the structure of knowledge in their discipline and who have opportunities possessed by no one else to observe learning in progress every day, can contribute greatly to the improvement of their own teaching and can also contribute to our understanding of student learning by becoming astute observers and skilled assessors of learning in progress.

Our selection of feedback measures for assessing academic skills and intellectual development required a framework that could accommodate outcomes specified by these various theories and research currents but that was primarily teacher-oriented.

To that end, the assessment techniques found in Section I are meant to provide information on skills and competencies identified in the latest developments in cognitive assessment but grouped in sets that we feel are familiar and useful to the average classroom teacher.

The first set of techniques assess mastery of subject matter, including competence in the basic skills. We have selected another group of assessment techniques to assess critical thinking and skill in analysis, and our third cluster consists of devices to assess creative thinking and skill in synthesis. The brief introductory note that precedes each cluster of assessment techniques is an attempt to bridge the gap between our organizing schema and those of other authors discussed above.

Assessing Subject Matter Learning

Four of the five classroom assessment techniques presented in this subsection aim at finding out what students remember and what they understand about a given topic. Three of those four techniques—Focused Listing, Memory Matrices, and Directed Paraphrasing—specifically assess what students recall and have understood about the subject matter presented in a lecture, reading assignment, series of classes, or other course activity. While Background Knowledge Probes are also meant to assess recall and simple understanding, this technique focuses on the students' prior knowledge of a topic, rather than what they've learned about that topic through the course.

Focused Listing and the Memory Matrix assess skills and competencies classified as "knowledge" in the Bloom taxonomy, "getting information" by the New Jersey group, and "knowledge acquisition" by the Pittsburgh conference. McKeachie et al. (1986) would characterize this rather low-level skill under the "cognitive" category of "learning strategies." Background Knowledge Probes take seriously Ausubel's advice that the most appropriate influence on learning is what the learner already knows, and it provides a way for teachers to determine that critical starting point.

Directed Paraphrasing draws on somewhat higher-level skills, as do Documented Problem-Set Solutions, the fifth assessment technique in this subsection. Directed Paraphrasing fits under Bloom's "comprehension" level; Documented Problem-Set Solutions fit under Bloom's "application," or what the Pittsburgh conference refers to as "problem solving." Both of these techniques require skills the New Jersey group classifies as "presenting information." Finally, the Documented Problem-Set Solutions are designed to assess and stimulate "monitoring"—one of the metacognitive skills identified by McKeachie et al. (1986).

It is important to recognize that these techniques are meant to supplement and complement, not to replace, the testing and evaluation teachers already do. By virtue of their dual nature, these classroom assessment techniques can and should be used to assess and, at the same time, to teach.

EASE-OF-USE RATING: I

■ **DESCRIPTION:**
Asking students to list ideas that are critically related to an important course topic is a simple, flexible way to collect feedback on student knowledge.

■ **PURPOSE:**
Focused Listing quickly determines what learners recall as the most important points related to a specific subject, topic, or lesson.

■ **SUGGESTIONS FOR USE:**
Focused Listing is particularly useful for assessing students' knowledge about a topic that has recently been presented in lectures, discussions, or assigned readings. Two appropriate times to use this technique are at the conclusion of class sessions built around textbook units or chapters and immediately after a series of related lectures or discussions.

■ **EXAMPLE:**
This Focused List is based on the definition of Subject Matter Learning given in the introductory material in this section:

Assessing Subject Matter Learning

Recall of Facts/Concepts
Definition of Terms
Organization of Facts/Concepts
Relationships Among Facts/Concepts

■ **PROCEDURE:**
Try this technique on yourself before using it in class.

1. Select a topic that the class has just studied and describe it in a word or brief phrase.
2. Write that word or phrase at the top of a sheet of paper as the heading for a focused list of related terms important to understanding that topic.
3. Set a time limit or a limit on the number of items you will write, or set both time and item-number limits.
4. Make a list, adhering to your limits, of important words and phrases you can recall that are subsumed by your heading.
5. Look over your list quickly, adding any important items you may have left out.
6. If you're still convinced it's an important and well-defined topic, give your students the same topic, tell them to make a "focused list," and give them time or length limits.

■ **ANALYZING THE DATA YOU COLLECT:**
Basically, you can compare the number of items (quantity) and the identity of those items (quality) on the students' lists with your own list. While your list should serve as the "master list"—the criterion against which to compare the students' lists—it's best to quickly skim a sample of the students' lists to see if they've come up with any items that you've missed.

■ **IDEAS FOR ADAPTING AND EXTENDING:**
To make this a more powerful learning exercise, you can do one or more of the following.
- Make your list available to the students afterwards for comparison and, if appropriate, discussion.
- Make—or ask students to work in groups to make—a follow-up list that combines the best of the students' lists with your own. This will provide feedback to the students about what's most important to learn, know, and remember about that topic.
- Ask students to write definitions for the terms on their Focused Lists.
- Have students turn their lists into expository prose, clearly explaining the relationships between the topic and the items and those among the items.
- Use Focused Listing again at intervals after the first administration. It then becomes a technique not only for assessing longer-term recall, but also for reinforcing and deepening learning.
- For even more specific information, consider using Background Knowledge Probes (Technique 3).

■ **PROS:**
- It's an extremely simple and quick way to collect information on a variety of topics.
- It gives the teacher a clear idea of which specific subtopics the students recall and which they don't, allowing for more focused and effective review.
- It can serve as a wrap up or pre-exam review to aid recall.
- If limited time is allowed for list making, it indicates what the most salient information is *from the learner's point of view.*

■ **CONS:**
- In its basic form, it requires only recall and so makes no demands on higher-level cognitive skills.
- Some students may be able to produce a list of relevant terms without necessarily understanding their meanings or interrelationships.
- If it's used too often or poorly, it can easily become a gimmick or a pro forma exercise.

■ **CAVEATS:**
- Try this technique yourself before using it in class.
- Choose a focus topic that is neither too broad nor too narrow. Whether or not this is an interesting and useful learning exercise for the students depends largely on the scope of the focus topic you choose. Choosing one that is too broad will lead to wildly divergent lists, while too narrow a focus can lead to extremely limited and trivial lists.
- Make sure both the task and limits are clear and that students know if you expect them to apply any particular criteria in generating their lists.

NOTES

NOTES

EASE-OF-USE RATING: II

■ DESCRIPTION:

A two-dimensional matrix—a rectangle divided into rows and columns in which the row and column headings are given but the cells are empty—provides easily collected and easily coded feedback.

■ PURPOSE:

The Memory Matrix assesses students' recall and skill at quickly organizing important course information into familiar categories using a matrix prepared by the instructor.

■ SUGGESTIONS FOR USE:

The Memory Matrix is useful for assessing student recall and comprehension in courses with a high information content, such as courses in the natural sciences, foreign languages, music theory, history, or law. It is best used after a lesson, lecture, or reading that focuses on a substantial amount of clearly categorized information. This kind of matrix can also be used, however, as a pre-instructional assessment.

■ EXAMPLE:

Several weeks after the introductory lessons on verb endings, a teacher wonders if students in the elementary Spanish class can quickly and easily categorize the verbs they've learned recently. She hands out the matrix pictured below and gives the class 15 minutes to fill the cells with as many different "base form" verbs as they can recall.

A Sample Memory Matrix for Spanish Verb Endings

	-AR	-ER	-IR
IRREGULAR			
REGULAR			

■ PROCEDURE:

1. Draw a simple matrix in which row and column headings represent important categorizing variables for the information covered in the lesson.
2. Fill in the blank cells yourself with the appropriate facts—in the form of words and brief phrases—covered in the relevant readings, lectures, or discussions.
3. Check to see that there is a good "fit" between row and column headings and the facts in the cells. Revise the matrix if necessary.
4. When you are satisfied with your matrix, draw a new one with only the row and column headings and spacious but empty cells. Duplicate this matrix on paper and hand out copies or draw it on the chalkboard and have students copy it.
5. Direct students to provide the information to fill in the cells. Ask them to write only words or brief phrases.
6. Collect the matrices and assess cell contents for the appropriateness and completeness of the information given.

■ **ANALYZING THE DATA YOU COLLECT:**
One way to analyze the data in the matrix cells is to first tally up the number of instances (frequencies) of correct items in each cell, then look for noticeable differences, both in total and average numbers of correct responses. It can also be useful to focus on the incorrect or marginal items, once again by tallying them and looking for patterns. You can also look for patterns in student performance: Who did well and who did poorly? If there are clear imbalances on student matrices that do not exist on yours, in terms of numbers of items in cells, it may indicate a failure to successfully recall or categorize certain types of items, or it may indicate that less instruction or study time was devoted to certain categories of information.

■ **IDEAS FOR ADAPTING AND EXTENDING:**
• Provide a matrix with missing elements other than the cell contents. Leave out one column heading, for example, but provide some cell information to serve as a clue to the identity of the missing column heading.
• Allow students to work in pairs or groups to fill in the matrix, providing a bit more time for the task.
• Fill in the matrix as a whole-class review by drawing the matrix on the chalkboard, eliciting the missing information from the class, and filling it in as you go. Ask a student or students to take notes, or write in the elicited information on the chalkboard or on an overhead projector transparency, and then assess it later.

■ **PROS:**
• It allows you to assess not only how many facts the students can recall about a lesson, but whether they understand relationships among those facts and can correctly categorize them.
• It produces a bare minimum of written information, so it's quick to read and assess.

■ **CONS:**
• By providing row and column headings, the matrix precludes the students from using their own categorizing schemes. This means the teacher may not find out if some students do indeed have different ways of organizing and storing information covered in the course.
• With very basic categories and information, it may be difficult to determine whether student answers represent what they've learned in the course or their pre-existing background knowledge.

■ **CAVEATS:**
• Start out with rather simple matrices, preferably no larger than two-by-two (rows by columns) two-by-three, or three-by-three.
• Provide enough space in the cells for a larger number of items than you expect.
• Give students a realistic lower limit for the number of items you hope they'll insert in each cell, but avoid giving an upper limit.

■ **REFERENCES AND RESOURCES:**
See Patricia M. Cunningham and James W. Cunningham (1987) for an introduction to the use of matrices to assess reading comprehension.

NOTES

NOTES

EASE-OF-USE RATING: III

■ **DESCRIPTION:**
Background Knowledge Probes are sets of simple, interrelated questions prepared by the teacher for use at the beginning of the course or prior to introducing any important new topic in the syllabus.

■ **PURPOSE:**
These simple question sets provide more detailed information about what students know about a topic than listing does. By sampling the students' background knowledge *before* formal instruction on that topic begins, these probes also provide feedback on the range of preparation among students within a class. Background Knowledge Probes are meant to help the teacher better gauge both the appropriate starting point for the lesson and the appropriate level of instruction.

■ **SUGGESTIONS FOR USE:**
These probes can be a useful way to begin a course, especially as the first assignment. The same or similar questions can then be used at the midpoint and the end of the course to assess changes in students' knowledge, clarity, and concision in responding. They can also be used to introduce multilesson segments of a course or important concepts that will run through a number of lessons.

■ **EXAMPLES:**
The following examples are two Background Knowledge Probes that could be used with *teachers* who are interested in assessing students' learning in their own classrooms. Example A focuses on knowledge of facts, and Example B on knowledge of experiences.

Example A:
1. Are you familiar with the "Bloom Taxonomy of Cognitive Outcomes?" YES NO
2. If Yes, list as many of the categories of outcomes as you can recall, and define or exemplify each.
3. Which of these outcome categories are most important to your teaching and why?

Example B:
1. Have you ever collected feedback from your students about a single class session or lesson? YES NO
2. If Yes, what is your most vivid memory—positive or negative—about the feedback you received from the students?
3. If you have heard of any assessment techniques used by colleagues—even if you answered No to question 1—do you recall one that particularly interested you? If so, please describe it.
4. What would you most like to find out about if you decided to use an assessment technique in one of your present classes?

■ **PROCEDURE:**
1. Before introducing an important new concept, subject, or topic in the course syllabus, consider what the students may already know about it— accepting that their knowledge may be partial, fragmentary, simplistic, or incorrect.
2. Prepare two to five open-ended or relatively open-ended questions that will probe the students' existing knowledge of that concept, subject, or topic. These questions need to be carefully designed so that, in asking the question, terminology that may not be familiar to the student doesn't obscure whether or not the student is familiar with the concepts.
3. Write these few questions on the chalkboard or hand out questionnaires to the students. Direct students to answer each question succinctly, in three to five sentences if possible. Make a point of announcing that these Background Knowledge Probes are *not* tests or quizzes and will not be graded. Encourage students to give thoughtful answers that will help you make effective instructional decisions.

■ **ANALYZING THE DATA YOU COLLECT:**
Once you've collected the responses, you might try dividing them up into three or four piles according to the degree of preparation for the upcoming learning tasks that the responses indicate. You could, for example, classify either the individual answers or the responses as follows: [-1] = erroneous background knowledge; [0] = no relevant background knowledge; [+1] = some relevant background knowledge; or [+2] = significant background knowledge. You could then try to decide what kind and how much instruction is needed by average students and what other kinds and how much more instruction is needed by the underprepared students.

■ **IDEAS FOR ADAPTING AND EXTENDING:**
To make this a more powerful learning device, try one or more of the following.
• If you have a small number of students, consider interviewing them and collecting oral feedback by taking notes or audiotaping.
• Use Background Knowledge Probes as a higher-level follow-up to Focused Listing.
• After students have responded individually to the probes, ask them to work in pairs or small groups to come up with mutually acceptable answers.
• Return the original responses to the students and ask them to write a new draft of their answers at the end of each class, each week or at any other logical, relatively short interval. After two or three drafts have been completed, ask students to write a brief commentary analyzing how their answers have changed over time.

■ **PROS:**
• These probes provide rich data not only about students' knowledge of the topic, but also about their skills in communicating what they know.
• They provide baseline data on which a teacher can make instructional decisions before instruction begins.

- They "prime the pump," stimulating the students to recall anything they may know about a topic before reading or hearing about it in your class.
- They encourage students to try to relate the lesson or course topic to their own knowledge and experience, stimulating the students to begin constructing their own personal "bridges" between old and new knowledge.

■ CONS:

- The responses can be overwhelming and even demoralizing if the feedback on students' preparation is at odds with the teacher's expectations.
- Through the process of analyzing and classifying the responses to the probe questions, the teacher may form slow-to-change first impressions of the students, which may affect the teacher's expectations.

■ CAVEATS:

Feedback from this technique can throw even the most well-planned lesson or course syllabus into serious question by requiring quick revision of instructional plans. Background Knowledge Probes should be used only if you have the time, energy, and willingness to analyze and respond to the information generated.

■ REFERENCES AND RESOURCES:

This technique, along with many other useful ideas, can be found in a publication put out by Roxbury Community College (1986). (See, especially, pages 8 and 9).

NOTES

NOTES

EASE-OF-USE RATING: IV

■ **DESCRIPTION:**
Students are directed to paraphrase a reading or a lecture, using their own words, for a specific audience and purpose, and within specific page-length or speaking-time limits.

■ **PURPOSE:**
The purpose of Directed Paraphrasing is to assess the degree to which students have understood and internalized a given lecture or reading by collecting feedback on their ability to summarize and restate the lesson in their own words.

■ **SUGGESTIONS FOR USE:**
Directed Paraphrases are particularly useful for assessing the students' understanding of important topics or concepts that they will later be expected to explain to others. For example, in courses in social work, public health, education or criminal justice, much of a student's eventual success depends on his or her ability to first internalize rather specialized and often complex information and then effectively communicate it to the public.

In pre-professional courses, specifying the audiences for the paraphrases can be particularly useful—especially if probable clients and supervisors are used. In more general college courses, especially in the humanities and social sciences, the audience might be other students in the class. Basically, the more authentic the audience, the more effective the paraphrase.

■ **EXAMPLE:**
One way to get a sense of how this device works is to try to paraphrase one or two of the other assessment techniques in this section. For example, try to paraphrase Focused Listing or the Memory Matrix for a colleague who hasn't read them. Limit your paraphrase to three to five sentences.

■ **PROCEDURE:**
1. Select a point in the course after a major reading assignment, lecture, group of related lectures, or other major instructional segment has been completed.
2. Determine who would be a realistic yet challenging audience for a paraphrase of this learning segment, and how much speaking time or writing space would be reasonable for such a paraphrase.
3. Direct the students to prepare a paraphrase of the chosen segment or assignment. Tell them who the intended audience is and what the limits are on speaking time or number of pages. Tell them also how much time they have for preparing the paraphrase.

■ **ANALYZING THE DATA YOU COLLECT:**
If you have collected written feedback, you could begin by separating the responses into four piles, labeled "confused," "minimal," "adequate," and "excellent." Then assess the responses by comparing the papers within and across categories. Another approach would be to circle the clearest and

muddiest points in the paraphrases, using different colored pens or pencils, and then look for patterns of clarity and confusion.

■ **IDEAS FOR ADAPTING AND EXTENDING:**
- Get an appropriate outside expert to comment on and assess some or all of the paraphrases and give authentic feedback to the students. The students themselves can role play the parts of the expert readers if necessary.
- Provide examples of particularly successful paraphrases or give each student a checklist of the strong and weak points of their work.
- Direct students to paraphrase the same segment for two very different audiences, and then to explain in detail the differences between the two paraphrases.
- Ask students to keep a journal of paraphrases as a summary of important points in the course.
- Assign different students to paraphrase different reading assignments or lectures and then to share those paraphrases with the other members of their study groups or with the rest of the class.

■ **PROS:**
- These paraphrasing exercises build on and build up the students' skills in actively and purposefully comprehending and communicating information learned in a course.
- They allow the teacher to find out quickly and in some detail how much and how well students have understood a given lesson, lecture, or segment of the course, providing direction for syllabus revision and course improvement.
- They force both teachers and students to consider the wider relevance of the subject being studied and the need to consider the needs and interests of the audience being addressed.

■ **CONS:**
- It can take quite a bit of time and effort to adequately assess the paraphrases *unless* strict length limits are enforced.
- It's quite difficult both to establish qualitative criteria for a good paraphrase and also to make those criteria explicit.
- The paraphrasing skills of individuals probably won't improve appreciably unless you do provide some focused and individualized feedback. Once again, this is a rather time-intensive technique.

■ **CAVEATS:**
For this to be a meaningful assessment and learning task, it must be well structured and planned. Students' first efforts are likely not to look much like their own words—most have, after all, had many years of practice in *not* writing in their own words. This device must be used more than once during the course if students, as well as the teacher-assessor, are to learn from the process.

NOTES

NOTES

EASE-OF-USE RATING: V

■ **DESCRIPTION:**
By asking students to document the steps they take in solving problems—to "show and tell" their work—teachers can elicit two types of valuable information on their students' simple problem-solving skills. This technique provides specific information about the students' success at solving problems and more general information about the students' approaches to problem solving.

■ **PURPOSE:**
The purpose of this technique is to assess both the students' ability to correctly answer the given problems and the students' methods of solving the problems. However, the primary emphasis of the device is on documenting the steps the students go through in attempting to solve the problems—rather than on whether the answers are correct or not. Understanding and using effective problem-solving procedures is, after all, critical to understanding subject matter.

■ **SUGGESTIONS FOR USE:**
This device is especially useful for assessing problem-solving in quantitative skills courses such as algebra, calculus, and statistics. It can also be used in courses in other fields in which generally accepted approaches to problem-solving are taught, such as accounting, microeconomics, tort law, organic chemistry, transformational grammar, music theory, or computer programming.

■ **EXAMPLE:**
Before leaving the topic, an Algebra I instructor wants to assess her students' approaches to solving quadratic equations. She goes through the procedure outlined below and assigns a three-problem problem-set as homework—directing her students to spend no more than one hour on the solution. The responses convince her that there are three groups in the class: those who answered the problems correctly and showed elegant form in solving them; those who answered two or three problems correctly but exhibited limiting or unclear form; and, those who clearly misunderstood the solution process and got most or all answers wrong.

■ **PROCEDURE:**
1. Select three or four representative problems from the homework problems students have been studying in the previous few weeks. Try to select at least one problem everyone can successfully solve, another that most of the class can solve, and another that is at the upper edge of most students' skills.
2. Rewrite those original problems, changing the details and rewriting them to make them as clear and focused as possible.
3. Solve the problems yourself and write down the steps you take in solving them. Note how long it takes you and how many steps you have jotted down.
4. If you find any of the problems too time consuming or too complicated, replace them with other more suitable ones. Revise others as necessary.

5. Once you have three or four good problems that you can solve and document in under half an hour, write them up for the students. Assume that it will take them at least twice as long as it did you to solve the problems while listing steps. Make your directions very explicit.

6. Hand out and explain the problem set, making quite clear to the students that it is *not* a test or a quiz. Stress that the point is to show *how* they try to solve the problems, and that their steps are even more important if they fail to get a correct answer. If you assign it as homework, ask students to respect the time limits.

■ **ANALYZING THE DATA YOU COLLECT:**

The feedback from Documented Problem Sets can be difficult and time consuming to analyze, but the information gained usually compensates the effort. One way to begin is by dividing up the responses based on number of correct answers—into three or four groups.

Then quickly sort the responses in each group in terms of your first impression of the quality of the work that's shown—not answers—from worst to best. Focus on only one problem in each group. Count the number of steps shown in that problem's solution in a sample of papers and calculate a rough average. Note the smallest and largest number of steps shown. Compare them with the steps you wrote down. Then look at the content and the order of the steps in that same problem, first for the students who got it right, then for those who didn't. Look for patterns in the solutions that differentiate correct and incorrect answers. It's often useful and efficient to analyze only a few responses in depth. If you choose to do this, however, analyze some of the best and worst responses.

■ **IDEAS FOR ADAPTING AND EXTENDING:**

• Ask the students to trade papers and analyze each other's problem solutions for number of steps. Ask them to try to follow those steps on their classmates' papers to see if anything is missing or unclear. Have the students return the papers and then review and rewrite their own solution steps for submission to you.

• Use this device as a diagnostic pre-assessment, limiting it to the easiest problem.

• Give students a follow-up set of parallel problems and ask them to use their own solution steps, or those of partners, to solve them. Ask them to note any difficulties in following their original steps or those of a partner.

• In response to student feedback, make up different handouts for different groups that emerge, based on their level of expertise.

• Divide the class into small groups and ask the students with elegant responses to explain their solution processes step-by-step to those who had difficulties.

■ **PROS:**

• This technique allows the teacher a look behind answers into the students' thinking processes and problem-solving strategies.

• It focuses the attention of teacher and students on the general skill level rather than on discrete, unique answers.
• It allows the teacher and the students to become aware of a multitude of possible successful and unsuccessful approaches to problem solving.

■ CONS:

• Students may find it extremely difficult at first to explicitly document their work.
• Teachers may not always be able to figure out or explain why a given set of steps works or fails to work.
• A great deal of time and energy may be required for preparation, assessment, and follow-up.

■ CAVEATS:

Don't expect students to write good step-by-step solutions the first or even the second time they try it. Most students have little or no experience in reflecting on their own problem-solving processes and so have to learn to do it. Don't feel bound to analyze more data than you can comfortably handle, but make sure that all students get some feedback.

■ REFERENCES AND RESOURCES:

In her very influential book, *Errors and Expectations* (1977), the late Mina Shaughnessey provided a comprehensive description and discussion of her experiences applying error-analysis techniques to the writing of underprepared college students. While she dealt only with writing instruction, her book remains the most thoughtful and complete statement on the use of error analysis to inform and improve teaching of which we know.

NOTES

NOTES

Assessing Critical Thinking and Skill in Analysis

Each of the four assessment techniques in this subsection is designed to assess students' skills at critically and analytically "breaking down" a large topic, question, problem, or text to understand it more fully and manipulate it more effectively. The devices are progressively more challenging, adding successive layers of difficulty in terms of the analytic demands they make as well as in terms of the communication of that analysis.

While the Defining Feature Matrix technique requires skills that Bloom would categorize as "application," and rather minimal output, the following classroom assessment technique raises the ante. Do & Say Analysis fits clearly into the Bloom category of "analysis" and requires critical reading and thoughtful writing from the student.

Both Focused Dialectical Notes and the Do & Say Analysis require similar reading and writing skills; the former, however, demands more critical thinking and active personal reflection than does the latter. This added dimension in the Dialectical Notes would be categorized as "evaluation," the highest-level cognitive outcome in the Bloom taxonomy. The Analytic Memo technique makes all these demands and more.

All of the techniques in this subsection involve what the New Jersey conference refers to as "manipulating information," and all but the Defining Feature Matrix involve "presenting information" as well. The Pittsburgh conference group would categorize these skills under "problem solving" and "intelligence and reasoning." Finally, under the rubric presented by McKeachie et al., these techniques deal with "thinking and problem solving" and, to a somewhat lesser degree, "learning strategies."

By whatever names we call them, critical thinking and analytical skills are central to academic success in most college programs. The techniques in this subsection assess and develop some of the higher-order skills that distinguish the well-schooled from the truly well-educated.

EASE-OF-USE RATING: I

■ **DESCRIPTION:**

By categorizing items according to the presence (+) or absence (-) of defining features, students provide data on their analytic reading and thinking skills.

■ **PURPOSE:**

This technique is designed to assess students' skills at categorizing course information according to a given set of defining features.

■ **SUGGESTIONS FOR USE:**

The Defining Feature Matrix is best used in courses that require students to distinguish between closely related or seemingly similar items. Some areas in which this skill is particularly important are biological taxonomy, geography, chemistry, astronomy, and medicine.

■ **EXAMPLE:**

Below we have used a Defining Feature Matrix to draw some distinctions between the general model of institutional assessment and our model of Classroom Research:

Features	Institutional Assessment	Classroom Research
Teacher-Directed	-	+
Teacher-Designed	-	+
Large Sample Sizes	+	-
Sophisticated Statistical Data Analysis Required	+	-
Standardized and Validated Instruments Required	+	-
Primarily Formative	-	+
Focused on Classroom Teaching and Learning	-	+
Replicable and Comparable	+	-
Useful to Students	-	+
Useful to Teachers	-	+
Useful to Administrators	+	+
Useful to Policy Makers	+	-
Aims to Improve Education	+	+

■ **PROCEDURE:**

1. Choose a limited number of items or classes of items that are similar enough to confuse your students.
2. Determine what the most important features are that the students must recognize to correctly categorize these items.
3. Make a list of defining features that each category either possesses or does not possess. These must be rather clear-cut in terms of their presence or absence, although the categories may share a limited number of features.
4. Sketch out a matrix with features listed down the left side and categories across the top, or vice versa.

5. Check to see that each cell in the matrix can be reasonably responded to with a plus (+) or a minus (-). If you cannot respond to the cell with plus or minus, the feature should probably be removed from the matrix. You can also use "yes" or "no" instead of plus or minus.
6. Draw up a revised matrix and give copies to your students or, if it's simple, have them copy it off the board.
7. Clearly explain the purpose of the matrix and the directions for filling it in, as well as the time limit for doing so.

■ ANALYZING THE DATA YOU COLLECT:

It's easy to compare the students' matrices to your master copy. You can scan them one by one, indicating incorrect responses on each student's matrix with a slash or an "X" and, at the same time, keeping a running tally of incorrect responses on a larger copy of the matrix with empty cells. You can also simply count up all the plusses and minuses for each cell and indicate them on an oversized copy. Look for those cells where students made the wrong choice and see if there are patterns in the errors. Are students paying more attention to certain features than to others?

■ IDEAS FOR EXTENDING AND ADAPTING:

• Make up a matrix with labels for the features but not for the categories, or with categories labeled but not features, and ask students to fill those in also.
• Present students with a sample Defining Feature Matrix on a familiar, course-related topic. Then ask them to create their own matrices to define categories or items related to a different important topic covered in the course.
• Work up to matrices that allow for more than simple binary responses in the cells. For example, for certain topics the features might be more appropriately categorized as "Always present," "Often present," "Rarely present," and "Never present."
• Ask each student to write brief statements explaining what the configuration of data in the completed matrix means.

■ PROS:

• This is a quick way to check students' skills at distinguishing between items or categories that are easily confused, and to pinpoint any areas of confusion.
• This technique gives students practice in using a simple, powerful and highly transferable technique for categorizing data.

■ CONS:

• This technique requires careful and thoughtful preparation, making it somewhat more demanding of teachers than of students. In compensation, it's easy to score.
• Not all information can be easily or accurately expressed with only a plus or minus. Many important definitions depend on differences in levels or degrees, rather than absolute presence or absence of a feature.
• If the matrix is not constructed to lead students to see important patterns of defining features in the data, then it can easily become a low-level assessment of their recall of isolated facts.

■ **CAVEATS:**
- Try to keep the features in the matrix parallel in kind or in level of importance.
- Don't include more than two or three categories or seven to ten defining features, at least in the first applications of this technique.

■ **REFERENCES AND RESOURCES:**
Patricia M. Cunningham and James W. Cunningham (1987) discuss the use of feature matrices and other organizational devices in integrated reading and writing lessons.

NOTES

NOTES

DO & SAY (FUNCTION & CONTENT) ANALYSIS

EASE-OF-USE RATING: III

■ **DESCRIPTION:**
This simple outlining technique provides information on students' critical-reading skills.

■ **PURPOSE:**
Do & Say Analysis is designed to elicit information on the students' skills at separating out the *communicative function* from the *informational content* of a text.

■ **SUGGESTIONS FOR USE:**
This technique is useful in courses focusing on written form, such as composition, literature, technical writing, or creative writing. It can be used in any field where there are standard forms for writing in certain specific genres such as the essay, the informational memo, the report, the business letter, and so on.

■ **EXAMPLE:**
The example below is an application of this technique to the material directly above.

Section	Does	Says
"Ease-of-Use Rating"	Tells reader how easy device will be to use	Moderately easy to use
"Definition"	Gives reader enough info to decide whether to read further	Simple outline to assess critical reading
"Suggestions for Use"	Tells reader what kinds of courses to use it in	Useful in writing-centered courses

■ **PROCEDURE:**
1. Choose a short text or a passage that is both structurally representative of a genre and that contains useful content.
2. If the structural subsections of the text are not clearly defined—by subheadings or numbers, for example—mark them clearly yourself. This is important so that all the students will break the text down into the same subsections.
3. Find a parallel text that you can use as an example and perform a Do & Say Analysis on it yourself.
4. Hand out your example text to the class and take them through your analysis step-by-step, modeling the process you want them to use. Many students find it difficult to understand and then express the distinction between function and content at first, so give several clear examples of this. Preparing a handout for them to study afterwards can be very helpful.

5. Once you're confident the class understands the technique, hand out the text they are to analyze. Go through the directions carefully and give them sufficient time to carry it out. Unless it is a very short text, this work should probably be done outside of class. Make sure to let the class know what kind of responses you are looking for.

■ ANALYZING THE DATA YOU COLLECT:

There are two main types of related yet separable data to be analyzed in the students' responses. The first is the analysis of the *function* of the segment within the larger text; the second, the related paraphrase of the *content*. A simple way to assess the class's understanding of the functions and content is to keep a running tally of the problem spots in the text—those segments students have trouble analyzing or paraphrasing.

■ IDEAS FOR EXTENDING AND ADAPTING:

- Ask students to use the same functions to express different content—a story from the news, for example—or to express the same content with different or differently ordered functions.
- Use this technique with several different types of writing and ask students to compare the functions used and the ordering of functions in those different examples.
- Take an interesting text you have analyzed and scramble the order of your analysis by cutting and pasting. Photocopy the scrambled version and give it to the students. Assess their skills at putting the pieces into their original—or another plausible—order.

■ PROS:

- This technique focuses on analyzing writing not only for content, but also for the functions of its component parts, allowing the teacher to assess the students' skills at seeing below the surface of the text.
- It stimulates thinking about patterns and common structures in writing, helping students see why different genres may encode the same information in different forms.
- This technique allows teachers to zero in on particular sticking points in text analysis, rather than giving them a global assessment of students' skills. It shows teachers what their students can do well and what less well, allowing for more fine-tuned teaching.

■ CONS:

- This is a time-intensive technique. Students may have quite a bit of trouble getting this, and many will not succeed at it the first time. It generally takes more than one administration to work well.
- Many texts are not particularly easy to divide up in neat and simple ways. Paragraphs or short subsections often have more than one function within a text.

■ **CAVEATS:**
Choose a clear, simple, and easily analyzed text for the first administration—as well as for the examples. Allow enough time to work through at least part of your examples, but don't feel constrained to do it all at once. This is the kind of technique that is often learned better if it is repeated over a period of days.

NOTES

NOTES

EASE-OF-USE RATING: IV

■ **DESCRIPTION:**

Students write Focused Dialectical Notes by directly responding to and questioning ideas and assertions within their assigned course readings. These dialogs, in the form of notes, can be used as a source of information on students' ways of reading and understanding course material.

■ **PURPOSE:**

This technique provides detailed feedback on how students analyze and respond to academic texts they are reading. By analyzing this information, the teacher can locate general problems in the students' analytic reading strategies as well as specific misunderstandings or problems with the content of the text.

■ **SUGGESTIONS FOR USE:**

This device is particularly useful for courses in fields where close study of texts is critical, fields such as history, philosophy, political science, literature, ethnic studies, women's studies, and law. The feedback can be structured in advance through the use of focused questions or this can be left to each student's judgment. To get the most useful feedback from Focused Dialectical Notes, the teacher may have to administer it more than once before students become adept at it.

■ **EXAMPLE:**

In a course on the theory and practice of bilingual education, the teacher assigns two well-written and highly opinionated essays—one strongly "for" bilingual education, the other just as strongly "against." In the margins of both essays, the paragraphs are numbered for easy reference. The teacher directs the students to read both essays quickly, then to go back and read each more carefully, writing Focused Dialectical Notes on each. The students use the paragraph numbers in their notes to identify those paragraphs to which they are responding.

The teacher collects the notes and skims through them, noting the paragraphs that consistently get the longest and strongest responses. He also makes notes on how the students are responding to what he identifies as the main arguments in the essays. He notes that the students often respond emotionally to key assertions but usually fail to go on to strengthen their comments with explanations, examples, or arguments. They also seem to ignore important arguments that they disagree with, rather than analyzing them and taking issue. More importantly, the students have great difficulty analyzing their own responses to the text. He decides to address these issues in class by demonstrating his Focused Dialectical Notes on the same text. He later repeats the process, noting some improvement in the second set of notes.

■ **PROCEDURE:**

1. Select an important passage from the course readings—one that is somewhat difficult but also relatively short and self-contained.

2. Ask students to divide a few pieces of notepaper in half lengthwise by drawing a line from top to bottom.

3. Direct them to take notes on the reading passage only on the left half of the divided notepaper. Ask the students to write down their reactions to the text—agreements, disagreements, questions, and the like. Suggest that they think of their notes as a dialog—a conversation with the text. Let the students know before they start that you will collect the notes and read through them but not grade them.

4. Direct them to return to the passage and their notes after a day or so, and then read through their notes with the passage nearby for reference. They will then write responses on the right side of the notepaper to their reading notes on the left side. Once again, encourage them to carry on a dialog with their own notes.

■ ANALYZING THE DATA YOU COLLECT

Once you have gone through the process of making your own Focused Dialectical Notes on a text, you can easily identify what you consider to be the key points. Check the left side of the students' notes to see how many of your key points get substantial responses in their notes. Look also for what they focus on that you did not. Then analyze the right side—their responses to their own text notes. Try to categorize the responses that students made to themselves, and then count the instances of each type of response. Look for changes in positions, reinforcements, qualifications, new insights, and the like.

■ IDEAS FOR EXTENDING AND ADAPTING:

• Ask students to take Focused Dialectical Notes on a lecture, rather than a reading passage. Make an audio- or videotape of the lecture for those students who need or wish to review it.

• Ask students to trade papers and to write comments on each other's notes.

• Have students turn their second-generation notes into an essay reacting to the passage.

■ PROS:

• This technique gives the teacher something akin to a reading protocol, a record of students' careful reading and reactions to a text. This can help the teacher understand how students read.

• It provides a contextualized sample of the students' skills at reasoning with themselves about a text, to think analytically about what they're reading.

• It promotes self-reflective learning as it provides feedback.

■ CONS:

• There is some danger that students will censor themselves or will try to write what they think the teacher wants to read, rather than writing candid, personal responses.

• Students often find this type of explicit response to reading unfamiliar and difficult, and often do rather poorly at first. This can be dispiriting to the teacher and the students.

■ CAVEATS:

This device requires skills that may be underdeveloped in many students. For this reason, it is important not to confuse a student's lack of skill in responding to a text and to his or her own comments with a lack of ability to think analytically. Your students may need to be trained in this reading and study technique, or others, before you can productively assess their analytic skills.

■ REFERENCES:

This technique is adapted from a teaching technique introduced to one of the authors by Dr. Dixie Goswami, a well-known writing teacher and researcher, in classes she taught at the University of Massachusetts at Boston during the 1984-1985 academic year.

NOTES

NOTES

EASE-OF-USE RATING: V

■ **DESCRIPTION:**
This short, structured writing assignment provides high-quality feedback on students' analytic and writing skills as a by-product of an intellectually challenging skill-building exercise.

■ **PURPOSE:**
Analytic Memos assess students' ability to analyze course-relevant problems with specific approaches, methods, and techniques. This technique also assesses their ability to communicate their analyses in a clear and concise manner.

■ **SUGGESTIONS FOR USE:**
Analytic Memos are particularly useful in any disciplines that clearly relate to public policy or management, such as political science, economics, criminal justice, education, environmental studies, business management, public health, and the like. This device works best if it is used more than once in the course and if it is first used early in the course.

■ **EXAMPLE:**
During the first month of an environmental studies course, the teacher decides to find out how well his students can analyze a typical environmental policy problem. He decides to capitalize on a local news story about contaminated groundwater. He directs the students to write an Analytic Memo about this topic. They write as environmental policy analysts and their audience will be the state's secretary of environmental affairs. The students are given one week to prepare their memos. After collecting them, the teacher assesses and responds to each memo with a checklist and short comments. From his assessment of the memos, the teacher sees that the students are generally successful at describing the problem and probable causes, but demonstrate little ability to analyze the policy implications of the problem and the interests of various actors and agencies involved. He then plans several lessons on applying political and policy analyses to environmental problems.

■ **PROCEDURE:**
1. Determine which analytic methods or techniques you wish to assess.
2. Locate or invent an appropriate, well-focused, and typical problem or situation for the students to analyze. Get background information on the problem or invent that information.
3. Specify who the memo is to be *from* and who it is *to,* as well as the *subject* of the memo.
4. Write your own memo on the subject. Keep track of any difficulties you have in writing the memo and how long it takes you from start to finish. Ask yourself whether it really required the type of analysis you were hoping to assess, and whether you found it interesting and informative.
5. Based on your experience writing the memo, develop an explicit, one-page directions sheet for your students. Specify the students' role, the identity of the audience, the specific subject to be addressed, the basic analytic approach to be taken, the length limit (usually two to three pages), and the assignment deadline.

■ ANALYZING THE DATA YOU COLLECT:

It's a good idea to analyze the memos for "content" (the breadth of the analysis and the quality of the information), "skill" (the skill with which the relevant tools or methods were employed in the analysis), and "writing" (clarity, conciseness, appropriateness of format, and overall writing quality).

■ IDEAS FOR EXTENDING AND ADAPTING:

- Provide students with guidelines for reading and evaluating each others' memos prior to rewriting those memos.
- Divide the class into "policy analysts" and "policy makers"; then have the latter group respond, in memo form, to the memos of the former.

■ PROS:

- The memos are valuable, realistic, and substantial learning exercises in themselves; they build and sharpen skills in addition to providing feedback for assessment.
- The memos provide rich data on the students' skills in applying analytic thinking and writing to a real or realistic problem related to the course.
- Since memo-writing is an important skill in many jobs, this exercise can also serve as an assessment of job-related skills.

■ CONS:

- Preparing the task is time consuming.
- Carefully reading, assessing and commenting on these short, two- or three-page memos requires a lot of time and concentration.

■ CAVEATS:

- To get good feedback with this device, choose a problem that is both real enough and rich enough to generate thoughtful analysis.
- The problem must also be familiar to the students or one with which the students can quickly become familiar.
- Give consideration to the amount of background material students need to prepare the memos.

NOTES

NOTES

NOTES

Assessing Creative Thinking and Skill in Analysis

This group of five techniques is the most heterogeneous and difficult to define of the fourteen in Section I. This shouldn't be too surprising, however, since creative thinking is a topic about which there's much speculation and little agreement among teachers, researchers, and theorists. What these five techniques do have in common is that they stimulate the creation—and subsequent assessment—of original intellectual products by promoting syntheses of students' intelligence, judgment and skills, and the course content. Thus, they all can be classified under Bloom's "synthesis" category.

Three of these techniques elicit written responses: the One-Sentence Summary, the Term Paper or Project Prospectus, and Invented Dialogs. The other two, Concept Maps and Annotated Portfolios, involve graphic or artistic expression allied with writing. McKeachie et al. (1986) advocate "knowledge structures," and techniques such as Annotated Portfolios and Concept Maps as simple ways to get at such structures.

Four of these techniques are aimed primarily at intellectual and academic creativity and the synthesis of concepts and ideas. Only Annotated Portfolios clearly invite a focus on graphic and visual expressions of creativity through paintings, drawings, and photographs. We recognize the need for more techniques to assess visual synthesis and creativity as well as techniques to assess other nonverbal forms of expression, such as music, dance, and athletics. To that end, we invite readers to develop new techniques to assess these skills and share promising ones.

EASE-OF-USE RATING: II

■ **DESCRIPTION:**

This technique requires the student to answer the questions represented by WDWWHWWW (Who Does/Did What to Whom, How, When, Where, and Why?) about a given topic, and then to synthesize those answers into a single informative, grammatical sentence—albeit a long one!

■ **PURPOSE:**

The purpose of this strategy is to find out how concisely, completely, and creatively students can summarize a given topic within the grammatical constraints of a single sentence. This is also a technique for "chunking" material into smaller units that are more easily manipulated and recalled.

■ **SUGGESTIONS FOR USE:**

This strategy can provide feedback on students' summaries of just about anything that can be represented in the declarative form, from historical events, to the plots of stories and novels, to chemical reactions and mechanical processes.

■ **EXAMPLE:**

In this example, the task is to summarize Classroom Research in one sentence. The matrix is provided as an intermediate step to the summary sentence.

Topic: Classroom Research

The summary in matrix form:

Question	Response
Who?	Teachers
Do What?	Assess
To What or Whom?	Their students' learning
How?	Using classroom assessment techniques and any other appropriate research tools and methods
When?	Regularly during the semester
Where?	In their own classrooms
Why?	To understand and improve learning by improving their own teaching.

The summary in sentence form:

Teachers assess their students' learning by using classroom assessment techniques and any other appropriate research tools and methods, regularly during the semester in their own classrooms to understand and improve learning by improving their own teaching.

■ PROCEDURE:

1. Select an important topic or work that your students have studied in your course and that you want them to be able to summarize.
2. Working as quickly as *you* can, answer the questions "Who Did/Does What to Whom, How, When, Where, and Why?" in relation to that topic. Note how long it takes you.
3. Turn your answers into a grammatical sentence that follows the WDWWHWWW pattern. Note how long that takes.
4. Give your students up to twice as much time as it took you to carry out the task, and give them clear directions on the technique *before* announcing the topic to be summarized.

■ ANALYZING THE DATA YOU COLLECT:

Perhaps the easiest way to organize the data from these summaries is to draw slash marks between each focus element of the sentence, separating the response to "Who?" from that to "Did/Does What?" and so on with penciled-in vertical lines. As you separate the components of the summary, evaluate the quality of each by writing a zero (0), a check mark ($\sqrt{}$), or a plus (+) above that element. Zero indicates an "inadequate" or "incorrect" element; the check means "adequate"; and the plus-sign indicates "more than adequate." You can then make a simple matrix to represent the whole class's responses, with the question-words as column headings and the three marks—zero, check, or plus—as row headings. Once you've totaled the responses, insert them in the cells of the matrix and look for patterns of strengths and weaknesses in the responses. For example, are your students better at answering "Who" and "What" questions than "How" or "Why" questions?

■ IDEAS FOR EXTENDING AND ADAPTING:

• Once questions of content have been resolved, ask students to rewrite their one-sentence summaries into concise, informative and elegant two- or three-sentence summaries. Have them share these rewritten but still very brief summaries with each other.
• Give students a few minutes to work in pairs or small groups to critique and improve each other's summaries—either before handing them in or after getting them back.
• Use this technique a number of times to summarize segments of the same book or subject, then ask students to summarize the entire book or subject in one paragraph by rewriting and linking their individual single-sentence summaries.

■ PROS:

• This technique provides a quick and easy way to assess students' ability to coherently summarize a topic in the fewest possible words.
• Students must organize the information they are summarizing within a familiar, useful, and memorable framework—the sentence.

■ CONS:

- Some material is not easily summarized in such a form due to multiple possible answers for some or each of the focus questions.
- Some teachers and some students may feel that "squeezing" a lesson or reading into this framework is an unacceptable simplification of the material studied.

■ CAVEATS:

- Don't ask the students to do this unless you have first determined if *you* can coherently summarize the topic in one sentence. It may not be feasible or appropriate.
- Limit the topic so that even if the material is complex, the summary task will deal with a manageable part of it. For example, if there are several main characters and actions in a chapter to be summarized, direct students to write a one-sentence summary by specifying which character to use as the subject of their sentences.
- Encourage students to make their sentences grammatical, factually accurate and complete, and original—but not to be too disappointed if they are not elegant at first.

■ REFERENCES AND RESOURCES:

In her book on composing, *Forming/Thinking/Writing,* Anne Berthoff (1982, pp. 70-79) presents a technique similar to the One-sentence Summary that she labels HDWDWW (How Does Who Do What and Why?). She offers it as a technique for organizing the chaotic information generated by brainstorming.

NOTES

NOTES

EASE-OF-USE RATING: IV

■ **DESCRIPTION:**

Concept Maps are diagrams that students draw in response to a stimulus word or phrase. The "maps" illustrate the associations students make between the stimulus and other words or phrases—the latter generated by the students themselves.

■ **PURPOSE:**

This technique provides an observable and assessable record of the students' conceptual schemata—the patterns of associations they make in relation to a given focal concept. Concept Maps allow the teacher to discover the relational schemata the learners bring to the task at hand—the students' starting points. It also allows the teacher to assess the degree of "fit" between the students' understanding of relevant conceptual relations and that of the teacher or the map common to the field or discipline. With such information in hand, the teacher can go on to assess changes and growth in the students' conceptual understandings that result from instruction.

■ **SUGGESTIONS FOR USE:**

This technique is useful in any course in which conceptual learning is critical, such as courses with a high theoretical content.

Before beginning instruction on a given concept or theory, teachers can use Concept Maps to discover what preconceptions and prior knowledge structures students bring to the task. This can help teachers make decisions about when and how to introduce a new topic—as well as discover misconceptions that may cause later difficulties.

During and after the lesson, you can use the maps to assess changes in the students' conceptual representations. Therefore, to most effectively use this technique, it's best to employ it before, during, and after lessons on critical concepts.

■ **EXAMPLE:**

One of the authors drew the following Concept Map in ten minutes, in response to the phrase "the purposes of classroom assessment techniques."

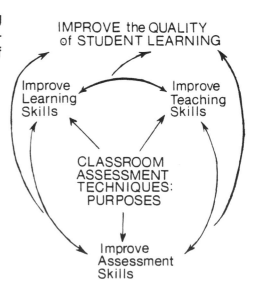

Classroom Assessment Technique 11
CONCEPT MAPS

■ **PROCEDURE:**

1. Identify the concept you wish to use as the stimulus, the starting point for the Concept Map. It should be a concept that is both important to understanding the course and relatively rich in conceptual connections.
2. Brainstorm for a few minutes, writing down terms and short phrases closely related to the stimulus.
3. Draw a Concept Map based on your brainstorming, placing the stimulus in the center and drawing lines to other concepts. One way to illustrate the concept is to make it roughly resemble a wheel with spokes.
4. After you've sketched in the primary associations, move on to add secondary and even tertiary levels of association, if appropriate.
5. Identify the ways in which the various concepts are related to each other and write those types of relations on the lines connecting the concepts.
6. Once you're satisfied with the "map" you've created, prepare a simple parallel example to use with the class.
7. Present the example to the class and work through it with them step by step, checking results as they go to make sure the process is clear.

■ **ANALYZING THE DATA YOU COLLECT:**

The results of this technique are best analyzed in terms of the content (the concepts) and the types of relations identified among concepts. Your own Concept Map can serve as the master copy for comparison. It's quite likely, however, that students will come up with some elements and relationships that you had not identified, so it is a good idea to review the data with an eye toward unexpected, creative responses.

The data can be coded rather simply in a matrix that juxtaposes *degree of relationship* (primary-, secondary-, tertiary-level relationships and so on) with *type of relationship* (set/subset, part/whole, parallel elements, cause/effect, defining quality, necessary condition, and so on). Once the data are coded, the numbers of responses in each cell can be counted and the balance among cells analyzed. Coding the data on 3-by-5 index cards or small slips of paper can make it easy to manipulate and rearrange.

■ **IDEAS FOR EXTENDING AND ADAPTING:**

• Ask students to list concepts within each "ring" or level of relatedness, and then to rank them to determine the relative distances within levels.
• Have students use large-format graph paper (for example, four squares per inch) for their Concept Maps. They can then determine and calculate specific distances between the focus concept and the various related concepts.
• Ask students to write explanatory essays based on their maps.

■ **PROS:**

• This technique reflects current research in cognitive psychology.
• This is a very "low-tech" way to get a graphic view of students' conceptual associations.
• It prompts students to consider how their own ideas and concepts are related as well as to realize that those associations are changeable.

- Concept Maps can serve students as pre-writing and note-taking devices in addition to being assessment techniques.

■ CONS:
- In-depth analysis of the data generated by this technique may require computerized statistical analysis.
- Comparisons among student responses can be very difficult to make unless the teacher restricts responses to choices from a closed list of terms. This, however, has the effect of restricting student creativity and the variability of responses.

■ CAVEATS:
- While students are likely to have some trouble identifying levels of association, they may have even more difficulty identifying the types of relationships among concepts. Going over a parallel example in class can clarify exactly what is expected of the students.
- Don't limit students' choices to a list of possible responses unless you are willing to constrain their creativity.

■ REFERENCES AND RESOURCES:
Louis Henry (1986) presents a very similar technique, which he refers to as "clustering," as an effective means of "writing and learning about economics." Novak and Gowin (1984) present a detailed discussion of concept mapping and other strategies for helping students learn in their provocative book, *Learning How to Learn.*

NOTES

NOTES

EASE-OF-USE RATING: IV

■ **DESCRIPTION:**

Students prepare a prospectus, a detailed plan for a term paper, or a design for a term project. The prospectus specifies elements of the paper or project such as the topic, purpose, intended audience, major questions to be answered, basic organization, and time and resources required. Students then write up the plan or design as brief, highly structured proposals before they begin substantive work on the projects they've planned.

■ **PURPOSE:**

The prospectus assesses the students' skills at synthesizing what they have learned about a topic and their interests in applying that knowledge to creatively and realistically plan their own learning projects. (The prospectus thus helps teachers assess how well students relate in-class work to assignments. In addition, it can give the instructor valuable information about the students' understanding of both task and topic before it is too late to make suggestions and shape direction.

■ **SUGGESTIONS FOR USE:**

This is an appropriate technique in any course that requires students to write term papers or to carry out substantial projects. It is most useful to students and instructors when it's used several weeks before the assignment is due. In fact, it's best to use it immediately after the assignment of the project is made to allow for adequate turn-around time.

■ **EXAMPLE:**

The example below is a simple prospectus format that can be adapted for almost any writing project.

```
                  Term Paper Prospectus

Directions:  The elements listed below are meant to help
you get started on your term papers.  Respond to each of
the prompts with a very brief, well-thought-out answer.
Remember that this is a plan, and you may change part or
all of it before you complete the term paper.  So, make
your best predictions and plans, but don't be worried if
you have to alter them later.

  Proposed Title:

  Purpose:

  Intended Audience:

  Major Questions You Hope To Answer:

  Proposed Table of Contents:

  Resources Needed:

  Calendar of Component Tasks:

  Your Biggest Concern(s) or Question(s) About the Paper:
```

Classroom Assessment Technique 12
THE PAPER OR PROJECT PROSPECTUS

■ PROCEDURE:

1. Determine the general outline of the term paper or project assignment for which students will write the prospectus. Write up the assignment in the form of a clear and informative directions sheet. These general directions should tell students how much freedom they have in terms of topic, form, content, purpose, audience, and the like. It should also tell students what criteria you will use to evaluate their final products.

2. Now decide which elements of the assignment are most critical to the learning task and which are least likely to be handled successfully by the students. Make a checklist of qualities or elements you will look for in the final product and rank them in terms of importance. Next, rank those same elements in terms of their difficulty for the students. For example, will the organization of the paper pose serious problems, or is choosing appropriate content the bigger issue?

3. Revise the general directions to reflect your priorities as expressed in the ranked list mentioned above. Check again to make sure you have left ample room within the structure of the assignment for independent and creative responses. Try to keep the directions to less than one page.

4. Now that you have clearly defined the assignment, you are ready to decide on the focus of the prospectus. Keep in mind both what you consider most important and what you suspect the students will find most difficult or least clear about the assignment. Compose three to five questions or prompts to elicit information about those central and problematic elements. These are the questions that students should *answer* in the prospectus. Invite the students to identify their questions and concerns about the assignment. These are the questions the students should *ask* in the prospectus.

5. Use the questions you've developed in Step 4 as the basis for a format or protocol handout on the prospectus. The students' prospectuses should be no more than one to two pages long and should answer each of your questions as succinctly as possible. They should also pose a small number of questions they need to answer before beginning.

6. Give out the general directions for the assignment and the specific directions for the prospectus at the same time. Ask students *not* to begin substantive work on the assignment until they have received feedback on their prospectuses. Give them a brief but adequate amount of time to do the prospectuses, from two days to two weeks, depending on the nature of the assignment and the course meeting times.

■ ANALYZING THE DATA YOU COLLECT:

In analyzing these prospectuses, look for the clearest areas and the muddiest. What questions or confusions come up repeatedly that could be clarified with the whole class? Which need individual responses? Are there groups of students who are working on similar projects who might benefit from a structured group discussion of their plans?

Note the range of topics and approaches in relation to your criteria for assessing the final product: Do you need to rethink your criteria, or do you merely need to explain them again more clearly to the students? Note also how and to what degree the prospectuses are related to the content and skills on which the course focuses.

Your brief comments on the prospectuses can be very helpful to the students—the more specific the comments, the more useful.

■ IDEAS FOR EXTENDING AND ADAPTING:
- Request that students propose only the title, purpose and major questions to be answered.
- Ask students to meet in small groups to present, discuss, and critically review each other's prospectuses before they begin work on the papers or projects.
- Make the prospectus the basis of a detailed outline of the project. Once the prospectus has been cleared, the student can move on to detailed planning.
- Have students write more complete and elaborated prospectuses for "dream" projects in the discipline that they would like to carry out in the future, but that are too ambitious or time consuming to carry out in your course.

■ PROS:
- The prospectus is a device that finds its own level. It can be as simple or as elaborate as the assigned project requires.
- It has immediate relevance to the student's work, concerns, and questions about the course. At the same time, it provides practice in a highly valuable and transferable skill.
- This technique gives the instructor both a preview of the students' interests and ideas and a forewarning of their problems and questions, allowing timely and helpful *formative* feedback. This preview of the final products also makes it easier to effectively assess them when they are completed.
- The prospectus reduces the likelihood that any students will totally miss the mark on the assignment by checking on their understanding early in the process.
- By requiring thoughtful planning, the prospectus improves the quality of the final product and enhances student learning.

■ CONS:
- The prospectus can tempt teachers to be too critical or directive too early in the assignment, increasing the risk that students will write more to please the instructor than to inform and instruct themselves.
- This technique requires a significant amount of planning and front-end work by the instructor, including reading and commenting on the prospectuses.
- Some students find it difficult to explicitly plan major assignments and may need coaching or instruction to produce a prospectus.

■ CAVEATS:
- Due to the time and work involved in carrying out this technique, it should be reserved for major term assignments. One prospectus per term is probably sufficient.
- You may make the assignment as open or as structured as you wish, but clearly, if you hope students will respond creatively to the assignment, there

must be areas in which you allow for and encourage creativity. Don't predetermine every aspect of the assignment.

- The directions should make it clear that a prospectus is a *plan,* a *forecast,* and so may be discussed, adjusted, significantly reworked, or even totally scrapped. Encourage students to take some risks, to propose something they really are excited about doing.

- Remember that many students have little or no experience in systematically planning their work. A poor prospectus, especially the first time through the technique, may not be a sign of poor ideas or lack of effort. It may be an indication that the student needs work in the very skills the prospectus requires.

NOTES

EASE-OF-USE RATING: IV

■ **DESCRIPTION:**
In the visual arts, assessment of portfolios is a common and well-accepted practice. Painters, photographers, architects, graphic artists—and even plastic surgeons and fashion models—often submit select samples of their work to potential employers, admissions committees, galleries, and foundations. Fiction writers, poets, and journalists also use portfolios of their work. In a somewhat different though related way, academic programs that grant credit to adult students for experiential learning often require or request portfolios of personal narratives, often supplemented by supporting documentation.

Annotated Portfolios combine the presentation of a limited number of examples of creative work with the students' own commentary or explanation of the significance of those examples.

■ **PURPOSE:**
Using Annotated Portfolios provides the teacher with a limited sample of students' creative work along with information on the students' understanding of that work in relation to the course content or goals. In essence, it allows students both to show and tell about their creative skills. At the same time, it allows teachers to see how students are connecting their creative work to the course content.

■ **SUGGESTIONS FOR USE:**
This technique has clear applications in courses in the visual arts and creative writing as well as in music, dance, drama, broadcasting, and clinical fields. In some of the latter, the students' "work" might be presented on video- or audiotape.

■ **EXAMPLE:**
Students in an intermediate drawing course are asked to submit an Annotated Portfolio containing two or three drawings in which they feel they have creatively resolved problems of line, form, shading, or perspective. Along with those two or three drawings, they must submit one to three pages of comments explaining how they creatively dealt with these traditional drawing problems and explicitly relating their solutions to the course content.

■ **PROCEDURE:**
1. Choose one or more central topics or problems dealt with in your course and invite students to respond to those stimuli with two or three creative works of their choice.
2. Ask the students to write very brief explanations of *how* the pieces in their portfolios respond to the stimuli and how they are related to the themes and content of the course.

■ **ANALYZING THE DATA YOU COLLECT:**
Annotated Portfolios can be analyzed from two complementary points of view. You may first wish to assess the quality of the two or three works in the portfolio in terms of creativity in resolving or dealing with focus topics or problems. Next,

you may consider the quality of synthesis demonstrated in the annotations. That is, read the annotations to assess how well students have synthesized course topics, themes, or problems into their own work and into their understanding of their own work. A simple ranking scale using letters or numbers will probably be adequate to provide a picture of the range of skills within the class. Taking brief notes on each portfolio while you rank it will provide you with a richer record, and a more useful one for later comparison.

■ **IDEAS FOR EXTENDING AND ADAPTING:**
• Invite students to add selected works to their portfolios as the course progresses and to re-think and re-write their annotations. This can help you and the students see and assess change and growth throughout the term.
• Ask students to choose the theme or focus for their portfolios rather than assigning it yourself. Require only that it be clearly related to the course content.
• Arrange an exhibition or showing of portfolios so that students can learn from each other's works and annotations.

■ **PROS:**
• The Annotated Portfolio elicits an active, self-generated response from students.
• It provides data on the students' images and conceptions of themes or topics central to the course that might not be as clearly expressed in prose alone.
• It requires students to go several steps beyond the creation of private images to explore and interpret those images for others.
• Annotated Portfolios can be playful and exuberant learning activities.
• They allow students to choose the work on which they will be assessed, giving the teacher insights into what they value and appreciate.
• The technique also prepares them to present their work to prospective employers.

■ **CONS:**
• Unless the technique is presented carefully and is well integrated in the course, some students may not consider it appropriately serious or academic.
• Students may spend so much time working up the components that they slight the task of interpreting the portfolio.

■ **CAVEATS:**
• There's a danger in over-assessing the portfolios: You may lose sight of the value inherent in attempting to express ideas in a fresh, personal way. An activity need not be *neatly* assessable to be worth carrying out—or assessing in broad strokes.
• It may be necessary to impose guidelines for the contents or the form of the portfolios. If there *are* to be guidelines or rules of any sort, make sure to state them clearly right from the start.
• Remember that this technique is designed primarily to assess creative thinking, not artistic ability or skill. The most beautiful portfolio may not necessarily be the most creative or thoughtful.

NOTES

NOTES

EASE-OF-USE RATING: V

■ DESCRIPTION:

When students invent dialogs, they synthesize their knowledge of issues, personalities, and historical periods into the form of a carefully structured, illustrative conversation. They may create Invented Dialogs by carefully selecting and weaving together relevant quotes from primary sources. Alternatively, they may invent reasonable quotes that fit the character of the speakers and the context.

■ PURPOSE:

Invented Dialogs provide rich information on students' skills at entering into the intellectual personalities and styles of expression of other people and periods as well as on their understanding of theories, controversies, and the opinions of others. This technique provides a challenging way to assess the students' skills at creatively presenting the material they have studied.

■ SUGGESTIONS FOR USE:

Invented Dialogs are particularly useful in humanities and social science courses such as history, literature, political science, philosophy, and contemporary issues. The teacher may suggest the topics, issues, or personalities to be dealt with in the dialogs.

Invented Dialogs can be invented in at least two different senses of the word. First, students can use these dialogs to speculate on possible but unrecorded conversations between contemporaries in a given situation within a given historical context. A student in a U.S. history class might create a dialog between an abolitionist and a slaveholder in the United States of 1855, for example. Or the students can juxtapose times and places, reinventing history to achieve an effect. A student of political theory might convene Alexander, Caesar, and Napoleon to discuss the difference between the leadership skills required to conquer an empire and those needed to maintain one.

■ EXAMPLE:

Setting: A faculty lounge in a medium-sized college.

Characters: Two college teachers. One is a Classroom
            Research booster (CRB); the other, a
            thoughtful skeptic (TS).

TS: Just why is it you think we all should put more time
    and energy into assessing our classes? Good
    teachers, and I happen to think I am one, are always
    assessing their students' learning. They've always
    done it.

CRB: I don't think we necessarily need to spend *more* time
     and effort on classroom assessment. I *do* think,
     however, that we can learn about our students'
     learning more effectively by using explicit,

focused, and systematic techniques. In other words, I'm advocating working smarter, not harder.

TS: But what about tests and quizzes? Aren't they explicit, focused, and systematic enough to assess students' learning?

CRB: Sure they are, when they're used well. There are still some important differences, though, between those evaluation techniques and classroom assessment techniques.

TS: Such as the names, you mean?

CRB: No, I think there's more to it than that. Tests and quizzes usually come at the end of lessons or terms, and focus on how much students have learned. Right?

TS: Yes, so?

CRB: Well, classroom assessment techniques, are meant to be used _during_ the lessons, while students are actively engaged in the learning process—not after it's over. Classroom assessment also focuses on _how_ and _how well_ students are learning; not just _what_ and _how much_.

TS: Aren't you just advocating testing earlier, more often, and better?

CRB: I suppose some tests and quizzes would work quite well as formative assessment tools. But there are a lot of other things I want to know about: things we don't usually test for and things I don't necessarily want to grade for.

TS: You mean you want to know whether your students like you or not?

CRB: Don't be snide. We all want to know that. But I'm thinking more about assessing some very traditional goals that I have for my teaching, like fostering a deeper appreciation for the subject and developing critical and creative-thinking skills.

TS: Amen. In your words, "We all want to know that." Even I have secret "higher-order" goals, but I don't think those kinds of things are assessable. I don't believe you can collect meaningful data on those sorts of things.

CRB: Well, maybe my project will change your mind. Let's talk about this again at the end of the semester,

```
               and I'll show you the results of my assessment of
               analytic reasoning in my classes.
```

```
     TS:   O.K.   I'll hold you to that, though.   I'll even
           bring an open mind with me.
```

```
     CRB:  Fair enough.   If neither of us expects miracles, we
           might both be pleasantly surprised.
```

■ PROCEDURE:

1. Select one or more controversial issues, theories, decisions, or personalities that are important topics in your course. Make sure you've chosen ideas or personalities that lend themselves to the dialog format.
2. To make sure you've chosen appropriate and stimulating topics, write one or two short dialogs yourself on the focus topics you've selected. These dialogs should be 10 to 20 exchanges long. Work up your dialogs as examples for the students to learn from. Note how much time it takes you to invent the dialogs.
3. If transcripts of relevant dialogs exist, collect a few and make them available as examples also. The "Melian dialog" in Thucydides' *History of the Peloponnesian War,* The Lincoln-Stephens and Kennedy-Nixon debates, Socratic dialogs such as the "Symposium," and contemporary philosophical dialogs such as the Chomsky-Skinner debates are all possible examples.
4. Make an instructive handout to help students get started. Suggest a few possible topics, give time and length guidelines, and list your criteria for a successful dialog. Make it clear to students that the object is to create an original, lively, persuasive, natural-sounding, and self-contained dialog.
5. Encourage students to repeatedly assess their own draft dialogs by reading them out loud before they put them in final form.

■ ANALYZING THE DATA YOU COLLECT:

In these dialogs you should look for the same elements you mentioned in your assignment handouts. You can, for example, simply count the number of important points that the students adequately address in their dialogs and rate the quality of reasoning expressed in the exchanges. Note whether remarks really follow and respond to one another, whether the exchanges are balanced, on-target, and in character. You can also rate them for literary qualities: Do they "breathe"? Are the lines speakable? Most importantly, remember to assess the dialogs for their originality, creativity, and success at surprising and delighting you.

■ IDEAS FOR EXTENDING AND ADAPTING:

• Have students work in pairs, with each individual responsible for researching one side of the issue but with both responsible for weaving together the dialog.
• Ask students to act out a few of the dramatic and original dialogs and present them live or on videotape to you and the class.
• Let students expand and polish their dialogs after you've assessed them, recycling them as the basis for a graded assignment.

• Direct students to translate the basic ideas and arguments in the dialogs into essay form

■ **PROS:**
• Inventing dialogs forces students to internalize and "process" course materials in profound ways, and it draws on higher-order thinking skills, often more effectively than term papers or essays do.
• This technique allows students a great deal of choice in generating, putting together, and selecting ideas.
• Invented Dialogs provide the teacher with information on both the students' understanding of course material and their creative skills.
• Invented Dialogs can provide students with a way to "get there from here": a vehicle for internalizing and personalizing theories, controversies, and concepts that might otherwise seem quite distant, abstract, and "academic."

■ **CONS:**
• Writing persuasive dialogs is hard and time-consuming work, both for students and teachers. Reading and commenting on them is similarly demanding.
• Students who feel they are not creative or not gifted at writing may resist the technique.
• Many students will have had little or no previous experience at constructing balanced, persuasive discussions of ideas—and even less at writing dialogs—and so may need coaching and encouragement.

■ **CAVEATS:**
• Don't be dismayed if the students' first efforts are less than totally convincing. Remind yourself and your students that this is a challenging task.
• It's easy to impose or suggest so many guidelines that the technique no longer allows creative thinking. Remember, the major point of this exercise is to generate an original, personal intellectual product.
• Begin with limited topics and modest guidelines. Any serious issue or controversy could provoke dozens or hundreds of exchanges.
• Make sure the examples you provide illustrate a range of possible topics and approaches. Sharing comments about your own experiences in writing the examples can reassure the students. Discuss the process you went through, the problems you faced, and the surprises you encountered.

■ **REFERENCES AND RESOURCES:**
Richard Davis (1981) presents convincing arguments for the use of student dialogs, well illustrated with excerpts from dialogs written by his own history students in Australia. In an appendix to the article, he also includes a dialog he invented to illustrate the usefulness of this technique.

NOTES

NOTES

Assessing Students' Self-Awareness as Learners and Self-Assessments of Learning Skills

Overview

The need for college students to be actively involved in their own learning has received a great deal of attention recently, especially since the publication of *Involvement in Learning* by the Study Group on the Conditions of Excellence in American Higher Education (1984). The general message of that influential report was that the quality of undergraduate learning could be greatly improved if teachers gave more attention to creating learning environments that *involved* students in their own educations. "There is now a good deal of research evidence," they wrote, "to suggest that the more time and effort students invest in the learning process and the more intensely they engage in their own education, the greater will be their satisfaction with their educational experiences, and their persistence in college, and the more likely they are to continue their learning" (Study Group, 1984, p. 17).

Metacognition is the term used by cognitive psychologists to describe students' understanding of their own learning skills, performance, and habits. Although the emphasis of various researchers differ enough to make metacognition a somewhat fuzzy concept (Brown, Bransford, Ferrara, & Campione, 1983), two broad aspects usually included are (1) awareness of and knowledge of self-as-a-learner, and (2) self-control and self-regulation of cognition.

Research suggests that good learners engage in more metacognitive activities than poor learners. Thus efforts to teach students metacognition have received some attention in recent years. The University of Texas, under the direction of Claire Weinstein, offers a course for undergraduates designed to help students learn how to learn. Weinstein and Mayer (1986) emphasize four activities that can be learned by students to help them become more efficient and effective learners.

1. **Comprehension monitoring** includes four types of knowledge plus some techniques or strategies for monitoring understanding. The types of knowledge that a student needs to approach a learning task constructively are (1) self-knowledge, including understanding of learning preferences, abilities, cognitive styles, etc.; (2) knowledge of the learning task, including knowing what is required (for example, type of test) and knowing what needs to be learned, that is, knowing what you know and don't know about the subject; (3) knowledge of prior understandings, including both the amount of prior knowledge and how it is organized; and (4) knowledge of strategies useful in the learning task.

    The second aspect of comprehension monitoring concerns the ability of students to *monitor* their learning while it is in process to see if they really do understand the lecture or the text. Examples of monitoring strategies are self-questioning, paraphrasing and summarizing, and transforming knowledge from the form in which it was presented to another type of organization. All of these monitoring activities help make students more active participants in their own learning and give them more control over their learning.

Several of the techniques presented in Sections I and II of this handbook call for the use of various kinds of knowledge and monitoring strategies. Matrices, for example, are techniques for transforming and reorganizing information; the One-Sentence Summary is a technique for paraphrasing and summarizing. In this section, Punctuated Lectures ask students to stop and monitor whether they are attending to learning.

2. **Knowledge acquisition** is a category used by Weinstein and Mayer (1986) to describe how students make knowledge their own—as opposed to passively absorbing information. Two strategies are believed especially important—elaboration and organization. Elaboration refers to activities that students might use to make the knowledge meaningful and therefore, memorable. The use of analogy, for example, transforms new learning into something familiar. The paragraphs on Ideas for Adapting and Extending used as a descriptive category for classroom assessment techniques throughout this handbook are examples of elaboration that deepen and extend knowledge about the assessment technique presented. The concept of organization refers to the student's ability to "chunk" materials into units that contain similar elements. Such organization makes the acquisition and manipulation of knowledge easier.

3. **Active study skills** benefit from all that has been said about the necessity for students to be *actively* engaged in learning; few educators remain unaware of its importance. But there does remain the question of how to help students develop active study skills. Planning, monitoring, and transforming knowledge are activities designed to give students more control over their learning and to make them more active participants. There are also, however, some *skills* that are basic to most learning—how to find the main idea in readings or lectures, for example, and how to relate ideas. Some of the techniques in this handbook *assess* whether students possess certain active study skills—Concept Maps, for example, require students to relate ideas, and the One-Sentence Summary involves picking out main ideas. In Section II, the emphasis is on whether students are aware of how they act on the learning task and whether they can accurately assess their own learning skills.

4. **Support Strategies** is a term used by Weinstein and Mayer (1986) to suggest that students need to assume some responsibility for creating and maintaining a climate—both physical and emotional—that is conducive to learning. Some students, for example, engage in negative self-talk ("I'll never be able to do it." "I'm just too slow to finish the test." "I'm...too old, too dumb, or too far behind."). Weinstein and Mayer believe that students can be taught to take control of their learning environments through monitoring, anxiety reduction, self-regulation, and similar strategies.

The four categories used by Weinstein to help students gain more knowledge of themselves as learners and thereby to take more active responsibility for their learning are all applications of the research on metacognition.

McKeachie et al. (1986) provide a good summary of recent research on meta-cognitive strategies, concluding that, among researchers, metacognition refers more to the control and regulation aspect of learning than to knowledge of person, task, and strategies that influence performance. Planning, monitoring, and self-regulation thus become the major activities that permit students to take control of their learning.

Planning activities, as defined by McKeachie et al. (1986), include setting goals for studying, skimming, generating questions before reading the text, and doing a task analysis of the problem. It is fairly clear now, from research, that good learners engage in such planning activities more often than poor learners.

Monitoring, as discussed by McKeachie et al. (1986), includes all efforts to monitor cognitive activity. These efforts include tracking attention as one reads, self-testing skills while reading a text to ensure comprehension, and monitoring one's pace and adjusting to time available when taking a test.

Self-regulation is related in some ways to monitoring. It permits students to make adjustments to the information gained from monitoring. For example, a student who finds that his or her attention is wandering while reading can reread, take notes, or use some other strategy to regulate and redirect attention. A student who is aware of the time pressures of an exam can use test-taking strategies, such as skipping questions and returning to them later, to gain more control over the situation.

There is not as yet much material available to college teachers on the concept and application of metacognition in learning. It appears, at this point, to be a very useful concept—and metacognitive strategies can be learned, or so a number of researchers believe. If these strategies can be identified and learned, it follows that we should be able to devise assessment techniques to measure the extent to which students possess these learning tools.

The techniques presented in Section II attempt to assess how aware students are of their interests and skills as learners and how capable they are of monitoring and assessing their own performances as learners.

Assessing Students' Self-Awareness as Learners

Students' assessments of the learning and growth they experience through participating in courses depend to a great extent on their images of their own starting points, skills, and capabilities, regardless of the accuracy of those images. This is one of the nontrivial reasons why students and teachers often disagree about how much or how little the former have learned. At the same time, students often know more about their skills and abilities than their teachers do— or at least than the latter can quickly and easily find out.

Students' assessments of the usefulness of their courses and their level of satisfaction with their own performance in those courses is also influenced by their individual goals. All too often, the instructional goals of courses seem to be based on one of the three following assumptions: that students' goals are identical to those of the course; that students' goals are irrelevant to those of the course; or, that students have no goals. We suggest that most students do have learning goals, although they may find it difficult to articulate them, and that information about student goals can be very useful to teachers in planning, teaching, assessing, and revising their courses.

In any course students are likely to learn more if they are capable of clearly articulating their goals and self-concepts and making connections between those and course goals and requirements. Self-awareness is crucial to involvement in learning.

Each of the techniques in this subsection focuses on student self-awareness of goals, interests, or learning strategies as they relate to classroom learning. The Student Goals Ranking technique is designed to help students not only to make their learning goals explicit but also to clearly rank them in terms of importance and achievability. Through Course-Related Interests and Skills Checklists, students make explicit their level of interest in the various topics dealt with in a given course and assess their proficiency and experience in skills central to success in mastering those topics. The third technique, Focused Autobiographical Sketches of Students as Learners, provides information on a single, course-related dimension of students' concepts of themselves as learners by asking them to reconsider past learning experiences in a new light. Dual Viewpoint Skills Portraits require learners to consider their skills from their own viewpoint as well as from the imagined viewpoint of a relevant "assessor"—whether teacher, supervisor, or client. By comparing how learners portray themselves from their own perspectives and from those of relevant others, teachers can learn about course-related aspects of their students' self-images and self-awareness.

EASE-OF-USE RATING: I

■ **DESCRIPTION:**

The Student Goals Ranking provides information on the learning goals students bring to a course, the relative importance of those goals to the individual students, and their estimations of the difficulty of achieving their learning goals.

■ **PURPOSE:**

The purpose of this technique is to assess the "degree of fit" between students' personal learning goals and teachers' course-specific instructional goals. It allows teachers to measure the "fit" not only in terms of content of the goals, but also in terms of students' rankings of relative importance and difficulty to achieve. Teachers can use the information this technique provides to help students make connections between their personal goals and course goals.

■ **SUGGESTIONS FOR USE:**

Student Goals Rankings are useful to all teachers interested in knowing what their students hope to get from their classes. The technique should be used as early in the course as possible, preferably during the first week of classes.

■ **EXAMPLE:**

The following is a list of goals one of the authors had for this handbook:

Importance	Goal	Difficulty
1	That it stimulate college teachers to experiment actively in assessing their students' learning	III
2	That the assessment techniques it contains be valuable to many college teachers in various fields	I
3	That it serve as one of the bases for teacher-directed Classroom Research	IV
4	That it make explicit connections between important currents in the research and the concerns of classroom teachers and students	II
5	That these techniques serve as the first draft of a larger, more comprehensive collection of classroom assessment techniques that can be easily updated and shared	V

■ **PROCEDURE:**

1. Make sure that you have clearly articulated your instructional goals for the class. If you haven't, go through this exercise yourself before trying it with your students.

Classroom Assessment Technique 15
STUDENT GOALS RANKING

2. Make your instructional goals clear to the class by handing them out with the syllabus and by briefly discussing them. Tell students how important it is that they, too, make their goals explicit, and that you'll devote a few minutes of class time to collecting that information.

3. Ask your students to take out a piece of paper and list three to five goals they hope to achieve by taking the course. These goals may concern bodies of knowledge, skills, sharpened perceptions, or appreciations. This step should take approximately seven to ten minutes.

4. Then direct the students to rank order the items on their lists in terms of their importance in their lives. One way to explain this is to say, "For example, if you could choose only one goal to realize, which would it be? That's number one. If you could the choose a second, which would it be? That's number two." Ask them to write those numbers to the left of the items on the list. This may take three to five minutes.

5. Next, ask the students to again rank order the list. This time, however, they should rank them in terms of their personal challenge level—how difficult the goal is likely to be for that individual to achieve. Ask them to use Roman numerals for this ranking, with I being most difficult, II next most difficult, and so on. Ask students to write these Roman-numeral rankings to the right of the goals. This step will probably take another three to five minutes. Lastly, collect the double-ranked lists for analysis.

■ ANALYZING THE DATA YOU COLLECT:

The most basic step in analyzing the data is to look for patterns in students' goals and categorize them accordingly. Since students are likely to have many of the same or similar goals, the challenge is to see those similarities despite superficial differences in individual expression. At the same time, however, you should look for goals that are truly different or unique and categorize them as such.

Once you have divided the goal statements up into a few categories and tallied the number of "votes" in each, compare those categories with your instructional goals. How well do they match overall? For example, are there categories of student goals that don't overlap with course goals? For those categories that do match or overlap, are the students' rank orderings of importance in line with yours? Do the students' estimates of difficulty fit with yours?

■ IDEAS FOR EXTENDING AND ADAPTING:

• Break the class into small groups and direct the students in each group to come up with a mutually acceptable group Student Goals Ranking.

• Ask students to rank order the list a third time, in terms of the amount of time they expect they'll need to realize each goal. Have them then create a composite "level of challenge" rank ordering that reflects both time and difficulty rankings.

• Do a follow-up in mid-course and near the end of the course. Look for changes in students' goals. Have they become more focused and realistic? More like the course goals or more different from them?

■ **PROS:**
- This technique raises students' awareness of their own goals, or their own lack of identifiable goals, in relation to their commitment to a given course.
- It allows you to see the degree to which students' learning goals overlap your teaching goals, information that's critical to gauging the students' level of investment in and motivation for a course.

■ **CONS:**
- Many students are used to accepting uncritically their teacher's goals and will find it difficult to articulate their own. Their first attempts will often result in general and vague statements.
- Students may express goals the instructor is unable or unwilling to address in the course.

■ **CAVEATS:**
- Don't be hesitant to tell students if their goals and your goals for the course differ. If they express goals that you cannot or will not address, they should know that from the start. If students know what to expect, they can make more informed choices about staying in or dropping and can more effectively focus their energies if they stay.
- It's a good idea to make some effort to respond to student goals. Try to adjust the course somewhat to address goals that, while not yours, are expressed by many students. This can be done by changing course content, allowing some alternative assignments, suggesting additional readings, and by suggesting other ways that students can use the course experience to fulfill their own aims.

NOTES

NOTES

EASE-OF-USE RATING: II

■ **DESCRIPTION:**
Course-Related Interest and Skills Checklists are simply brief, teacher-made versions of the commercial interest and skills inventories long used by guidance and career counselors. Teachers create checklists of topics covered in their courses and skills strengthened by or required for succeeding in those courses. Students rate their interest in the various topics and assess their level of skill or knowledge by circling the appropriate responses on the checklist. The students' two-fold response can provide insights into self-awareness that a simple interest inventory might not.

■ **PURPOSE:**
The purpose of these checklists is to inform teachers of their students' level of interest in course topics and self-assessment of skills and knowledge needed for or strengthened by the course. With such information, teachers can better plan and adjust their teaching agendas. They can plan how best to approach topics about which students indicated particularly high or low interest. They can also adjust their syllabi to take into account students' self-assessed skills and knowledge levels.

■ **SUGGESTIONS FOR USE:**
Like Student Goals Ranking, this technique works best if used as early in the term as possible. It can then be readministered midway through and near the end of the course to provide information on changes in interests and skills assessments related to course activities.

■ **EXAMPLE:**
The sample checklist that follows contains a list of topics as well as relevant skills that might be considered in a course on Classroom Research.

SAMPLE COURSE-RELATED INTERESTS AND SKILLS CHECKLIST

"Introduction to Classroom Research for College Teachers"

Part I: Interest in Course-Related Topics

Directions: Please circle the number after each of the items below to best represent your level of interest in that topic. The numbers are codes for these responses.

   0 - No interest in the topic
   1 - Interested in an overview of the topic
   2 - Interested in reading and listening to materials on this topic
   3 - Interested in doing a research paper or research project on this topic

Classroom Assessment Technique 16
COURSE-RELATED INTEREST AND SKILLS CHECKLISTS

Topics:
1. Teacher Effectiveness	0	1	2	3
2. Teacher Evaluation	0	1	2	3
3. Structured Observation of Classrooms	0	1	2	3
4. Teachers' Goals	0	1	2	3
5. Faculty Development	0	1	2	3
6. Teaching Tips	0	1	2	3
7. Learning Styles	0	1	2	3
8. (Behavioral) Instructional Objectives	0	1	2	3
9. Classroom Test Construction	0	1	2	3
10. Study Skills and Learning Skills	0	1	2	3
11. Teacher/Student Self-Assessments	0	1	2	3
12. Survey Questionnaire Construction	0	1	2	3

Part II: Self-Assessment of Course-Related Skills

Directions: In this part of the checklist, please circle the letter that best represents your assessment of your skills and experience in the areas listed below. The numbers in parentheses refer to the topics in Part I. The key to the letters follows.

N – No skills/No Experience
R – Rudimentary Skills/Very Little Experience
F – Functionally Adequate Skills/Some Experience
A – Advanced Skills/Extensive Experience

Classroom Test Construction (9)	N	R	F	A
Simple Descriptive Statistics (10)	N	R	F	A
Self-Observation (11)	N	R	F	A
Peer Observation (2)	N	R	F	A
Survey Questionnaire Construction (12)	N	R	F	A
Analyzing Videotaped Classes (3)	N	R	F	A
Analyzing Transcripts of Classes (3)	N	R	F	A
Writing Behavioral Objectives (8)	N	R	F	A
Analyzing Learning Style (7)	N	R	F	A

■ PROCEDURE:

1. Make two lists. The first will be a list of the main topics your course will deal with; the second, a list of the skill required of students or to be acquired by students through the course.
2. Come up with a simple, useful, and appropriate way to code student responses. (For many teachers, the codes in the sample checklist above can serve as models.)
3. Make a draft checklist that contains the edited contents of both lists and the related coding schemes. Try the draft version out yourself, then revise it as required. Make up a final version of the checklist that's easy to use and easy to code.

■ ANALYZING THE DATA YOU COLLECT:

Tallying the responses for each item is the simplest way to organize the data, and it is more informative than calculating the average (mean) responses. By doing this you can easily see which items received significant numbers of very low or very high ratings. Then cluster the interests and skills into related groups and plot their values on a graph. Plotting parallel bar graphs to indicate interest levels for Topic X and self-assessed skill/experience ratings for related Skill X can be informative to both teachers and students.

■ IDEAS FOR EXTENDING AND ADAPTING:

• Ask students to comment on the two or three topics they are most—or least—interested in and explain the focus and motivation of their interests in detail. Have them do the same for the skills they rate lowest or highest.
• Demonstrate how students themselves can discover mismatches and good fits between their interests and their skills and experiences. Ask them to take the checklists away from class, analyze them, and comment on one mismatch and how they intend to turn it into a good fit.
• Use a graphic display to show the areas of overlap and fit between student interests and skills and the course topics and requirements.

■ PROS:

• Course-Related Interests and Skills Checklists make it possible for the teacher to differentiate those course topics students are motivated to learn from those they are not, and those course-related skills students feel competent in from those they do not. This kind of information allows the teacher to plan strategically to devote more or less effort and time to different segments of the syllabus in relation to student needs, interests, and abilities.
• This technique promotes self-assessment and awareness in the students who use it. It requires that they consider their interests and skills in explicit relation to the course at hand.
• It gives teachers information on the students' self-concepts of course-related skills. The teacher can compare the students' self-assessments with his or her own to learn how closely they agree.

■ CONS:
- Preparing a checklist can be rather time consuming. This "front-end" investment is offset by the fact that it takes very little time to administer or code.
- The interests and skills levels students self-report may not fit teachers' hopes or plans, requiring them to choose either to ignore the checklist results or redesign the course.

■ CAVEATS:
- The fact that students don't express interest in a given topic doesn't mean that they cannot or will not develop interest in that topic through the course. It is often the case, as the old saying goes, that "Knowledge breeds enthusiasm."
- In many courses, especially those at the introductory or beginning levels, students' self-assessments of skills may provide more accurate and useful information about their self-confidence than about their proficiencies.

NOTES

FOCUSED AUTOBIOGRAPHICAL SKETCHES OF STUDENTS AS LEARNERS

EASE-OF-USE RATING: IV

■ **DESCRIPTION:**

At one time or another, most college students have been asked to write personal statements or autobiographical essays. Such written self-portraits are often a required part of applications for admission and for scholarships, for example. The Focused Autobiographical Sketch is simply a shorter and more specific version of these familiar tasks. In this technique, students are directed to write a one- to three-page autobiographical sketch focused on a single learning experience in their past—an experience relevant to the particular course in which the technique is used.

■ **PURPOSE:**

The Focused Autobiographical Sketch provides information on the students' self-concept and self-awareness as learners within a specific field. It gives the teacher a composite portrait of the range and diversity of levels of self-awareness and reflectiveness among students in the class. This information can help the teacher determine "where the students are" in order to more effectively gauge the appropriate level of instruction and set realistic course objectives. These sketches can also provide "starting-line" information against which to assess learning over the course of the semester.

■ **SUGGESTIONS FOR USE:**

The kinds of autobiographical writing referred to in the Description above are used primarily for selection and gate-keeping. Focused Autobiographical Sketches, on the other hand, should only be used for diagnostic and formative evaluation. This technique is appropriate for all courses having goals of positive growth in self-confidence, self-awareness, and self-assessment for students.

■ **EXAMPLE:**

In a graduate course on leadership skills for mid-career public administrators, one of the instructor's central objectives is to help her students become more explicitly and critically aware of their preconceptions about leadership, individual leadership styles, and how people learn to lead. In an attempt to determine an appropriate starting point for the class, as well as to collect a kind of "pre-test" data for later comparison, she asks each student, during the first week of class, to write a two- to three-page Focused Autobiographical Sketch. The focus of the sketch is on an attempt by the student to exercise leadership in a public situation and what he or she learned through it. The specific assignment is as follows:

```
Write a two- to three-page autobiographical sketch
relating and discussing an experience in which you
tried to exercise leadership in a public context and
learned something significant from the attempt—
whether you succeeded at leading or not. Focus not
only on what you learned but how and why you
learned from that particular experience. What does
it tell you about your ways of learning?
```

FOCUSED AUTOBIOGRAPHICAL SKETCHES OF STUDENTS AS LEARNERS

■ **PROCEDURE:**
1. Determine what element or elements of the students' learning experiences you want to focus the sketch on. Limit the scope of the focus and make sure it is directly related to the course goals and objectives.

2. Limit the sketch still further by determining what period or periods in the students' lives and what specific areas of their lives—for example, professional, academic, or interpersonal—the sketch should cover.

3. Consider what scale, if any, or criteria you will use to assess the sketches. Then reconsider your focus in the light of your assessment criteria: Does it still make sense?

4. If the answer to the above question is Yes, construct very explicit directions for the students to follow in writing the Focused Autobiographical Sketch. Since it is important these be short, the more limited the field of concern is, the better.

■ **ANALYZING THE DATA YOU COLLECT:**
Since the aim of this technique is to gather well-focused information on certain relevant student learning experiences, the analysis of data should be limited to categorizing and counting those experiences in ways that will help you better focus the class. You may simply categorize the experiences recounted as relevant or not relevant to the course content, and then further break down the "relevant" category into subcategories such as directly, indirectly, and tangentially relevant. Alternatively, you could categorize the reported experiences in terms of duration or frequency. A third approach is to evaluate the quality or intensity of the experiences recounted. A fourth option is to assess the level of self-awareness or critical reflection displayed in the sketches.

■ **IDEAS FOR EXTENDING AND ADAPTING:**
• As a follow-up, ask students to explain the criteria they applied in judging the experiences they've chosen to write about: Why did they consider the experiences successes or failures? Positive or negative?
• Direct students to focus on the same experience from the point of view of another person who was involved or one who might have been.

■ **PROS:**
• Focused Autobiographical Sketches allow teachers to assess only those dimensions of the students' experiences likely to be relevant to the course content and goals.
• This technique provides information on the range and diversity of past experience and level of self-awareness within a class. This information can be used for setting instructional goals appropriate to the particular students in the course.

FOCUSED AUTOBIOGRAPHICAL SKETCHES OF STUDENTS AS LEARNERS

■ **CONS:**
- There are no simple, widely accepted guidelines on how to judge the quality or intensity or value of learning experience, so this technique requires that teachers develop their own.
- Reading such sketches, even very brief ones, requires a lot of time and attention, as does responding to them in even the simplest ways.

■ **CAVEATS:**
- Many students are relatively proficient at narrating their past experience but unskilled at critically assessing it. Such students may need instruction and guidance in writing critical, reflective prose, and especially in focusing their writing, before their sketches will yield much useful information.

NOTES

NOTES

DUAL-VIEWPOINT SKILLS PORTRAITS

EASE-OF-USE RATING: V

■ DESCRIPTION:

Moving a step beyond Focused Autobiographical Sketches, which provide information on students' self-assessment of course-related past experiences, Dual-Viewpoint Skills Portraits ask students to assess their present levels of development in course-related skills from more than one point of view. Since different courses aim at developing different skills, abilities or qualities, teachers need information on students' self-awareness as learners in relation to those different dimensions. As the name suggests, however, these brief self-portraits require that students try to assess their skills from the viewpoint of another person. That other person may be a client, patient, customer, student, teacher, coach, supervisor, or mentor. The students' attempts to "de-center," to see themselves as another might see them, can provide rich information about their self-images as learners.

■ PURPOSE:

These portraits provide information of two types. First, this technique allows the teacher to match the students' two different "self" portraits against his or her own evaluation of their skills. Second, it provides information about students' skills at self-assessing and imagining how others might assess them in terms of those same skills. It is the second type of information that is of principal interest to the assessment of students' self-awareness as learners. Consequently, this technique aims both at assessing and at raising self-awareness in students and at making them more adept at assessing their skills as others do.

■ SUGGESTIONS FOR USE:

This technique is most useful in courses focusing heavily on skills in fields that demand highly accurate self-awareness and grounded self-confidence in successful practitioners. In other words, it's appropriate for any course that prepares students to exercise their skills in public settings, to "perform" publicly. Examples of fields that prepare students for such public performance are medical sciences, legal studies, education, finance and accounting, broadcast journalism, and many service-sector vocational training courses.

■ EXAMPLE:

In a large university's math department, graduate students who teach sections of freshman-level and sophomore-level courses are required to participate in a teaching skills seminar. As part of this seminar, each of the graduate teaching fellows is videotaped while teaching a section at the beginning of the term and near the middle. The master teacher leading the seminar asks each teaching fellow to view his or her video alone and then to write two brief, parallel skills portraits describing what they've seen. The first portrait is from the teaching fellow's own point of view as a teacher; the second is from the (imagined) point of view of an intelligent and observant student who knows very little about the subject and has very average math abilities. Both portraits should focus on describing instances in which the teaching fellow was using one or more of the following three skills: transmitting information clearly, encouraging active and engaged participation, and helping students make connections between old and new knowledge. The seminar leader directs the teaching fellows to limit themselves as much as possible to description and to write no more than one to two pages for each portrait. After the master teacher has read the two portraits, he or she and the teaching fellow view the videotape together. The comments from the two portraits form the basis for a shared discussion of the teaching performance on tape.

■ PROCEDURE:

1. Identify one or more skills that your students must prepare to exercise in public and that your course is designed to strengthen.
2. Determine how and when the students can observe themselves in the act of demonstrating those skills. Can they use videotape, audiotape, process notes, or post hoc recall?
3. Decide on one or more relevant points of view for students to consider besides their own. You may assign the other viewpoint or allow students to choose from a limited number of relevant others.
4. Give the students fairly specific guidelines as to what kinds of skills to focus on, what points of view to write from, and how long and detailed each portrait should be.
5. Direct students to assess their performance of the focus skill(s) only after they have described that performance. Ask them to assess each skill performance from both points of view as "Ineffective," "Adequate," or "Very Effective."

■ ANALYZING THE DATA YOU COLLECT:

The main purposes of analyzing these portraits are to assess the degree to which students are able to describe and assess their skills from their own viewpoints and to assess how well they can imagine and empathize with the viewpoints of those who will be affected by their skilled performance. While it will be useful to aggregate the students' individual assessments and compare self versus "other" ratings, the most meaningful criteria for analyzing these portraits must be based largely on the teacher's expert knowledge and judgment. It's both necessary and useful, then, to quickly and simply rate the students' portraits in terms of relevant criteria, such as accuracy of observation, clarity of description, accuracy of self-assessment, and accuracy of "other" assessment.

■ IDEAS FOR EXTENDING AND ADAPTING:

• When students have successfully learned this technique, ask them to take the next step and diagnose their own performances and suggest ways to improve them.

■ PROS:

• Dual-Viewpoint Skills Portraits encourage students to try to monitor their performances from the viewpoints of their relevant "audiences" as well as from their own viewpoints.

- The technique provides teachers with information on students' self-awareness, ability to objectively self-monitor, and with criteria for performing important course-related skills.
- The portraits themselves can also be used as the basis for one-on-one advising or coaching sessions with the students.

■ CONS:

- Dual-Viewpoint Skills Portraits require much self-reflective effort from the students and careful reading from the teachers. As a consequence, it's a time- and labor-intensive technique.

■ CAVEATS:

- Make sure that the focus of the technique is on skills, an alterable variable, and not on personal and relatively unalterable variables such as personality or basic communicative style.
- Don't expect novice or apprentice practitioners to notice much about their own performances at first. Most people find it much easier to judge their performances than to describe them carefully.
- Try to focus most of the attention on positive behaviors that can be improved in the course of the class.

NOTES

NOTES

Assessing Students' Self-Assessments of Learning Skills

These four simple techniques encourage students to assess their own learning skills. At the same time, they allow teachers both to see those skills through their students' eyes and also to assess their students' skills at self-assessment. Each technique focuses on an important learning skill, mastery of which can greatly increase the students' success in learning.

Self-Studies of Engaged Learning Time allow students and teachers to assess the students' skills at estimating learning time needed and at staying on track. Through this technique, both students and teachers can observe the total amount of time and the subtotal of active "time on task" students actually spend carrying out a particular assignment. The Punctuated Lecture technique provides students with a structured opportunity to assess how and how well they listen to and learn from lectures by focusing their attention on what they are doing and thinking about as the lecturer speaks. Process Self-Analysis focuses on the component steps the student goes through in completing an assignment, allowing teacher and student to zero in on faulty or missing steps in the student's work process. The final technique in the set, Self-Diagnostic Learning Logs, requires students to assess their own learning diagnostically. Once again, this technique not only provides information about the students' learning skills and ability to self-assess, but also encourages the development of positive meta-cognitive learning strategies.

SELF-STUDIES OF ENGAGED LEARNING TIME

EASE-OF-USE RATING: II

■ DESCRIPTION:
This sample technique encourages students to estimate, monitor, document, and reflect on how effectively they use academic learning time. Focusing on one assignment, class session, or activity, students estimate the amount of *Engaged Learning Time* (time spent actively learning) that they will devote to that task. They then monitor their actual time use, stopping every ten to fifteen minutes to note how many of those minutes were really spent engaged in active learning. Finally, they reflect on the differences, if any, between their estimated and real engaged time-use and draw their own conclusions from these results. Students then write very brief, anonymous reports on the results of their self-studies.

■ PURPOSE:
From the teacher's point of view, the purpose of these self-studies of engaged learning time is primarily diagnostic. They provide data on how much time students spent actively engaged in a particular learning task, and what fraction that engaged time was of the total time students devoted to the task. From these simple figures, teachers can learn about the range of total time and engaged time students are devoting to learning tasks, as well as about students' skill at estimating time use and effective monitoring themselves. Teachers can use such data to inform decisions about assignment length and structure, whether or not to teach study skills, and overall course pacing and workload.

From the students' point of view, the main purpose of this technique is self-help! Discovering how effectively they estimate and use academic learning time can give them more control over their study patterns. That control, in turn, can help them to improve their skills at estimating, monitoring, and self-regulating their learning time. Improved metacognitive learning skills pay off in more effective and efficient learning, which leads to less stress and more success.

■ SUGGESTIONS FOR USE:
This technique is particularly useful in courses that make heavy, ongoing time demands on students or in courses in which students complain about excessive time demands. At the same time, this technique will provide interesting and useful data in virtually any course for which students have a number of relatively short assignments.

■ EXAMPLE:
The instructor in a statistics course, dismayed by his students' complaints that his assignments took unreasonable amounts of time to complete, asked them to do self-studies of engaged learning time as part of their next assigned problem set.

After giving the students a few minutes to look over the problem set, he asked them to write down estimates of two things: the total time they would spend on the assignment and the subtotal of productive, active engaged learning time they would spend on it. He then gave each student a stack of index cards and directed them to stop every fifteen minutes or so, note the time, and honestly evaluate how much of the time since last note had been spent "on task." He advised them to tape a note reminding them to stop every fifteen minutes to the wall in front of them or to the computer screen as they studied.

He asked them to keep careful track of the total time spent and engaged time spent and then to write up a brief, anonymous report on a form he handed out for that purpose. The form is reproduced below:

A Self-Study of Engaged Learning Time

1.

	Total time	Engaged time	Difference (+/−)
Estimate	_____	_____	_____
Actual time	_____	_____	_____

2. What was the most interesting, surprising and/or useful thing you learned through this self-study exercise? (Please answer in five to seven sentences).

■ PROCEDURE:

1. Decide what the focus of the self-study will be. You may ask students to focus on a homework assignment, a paper, a problem set, a study-group meeting, or even a lecture.

2. Ask students to estimate both the *total* time they will spend on the focus task and the engaged, active learning time they will spend on it. Explain what you mean by engaged time and give examples. Come up with your own estimates for later comparison.

3. Direct students to stop and make note of their engaged time use every fifteen to twenty minutes as they work. Give them some suggestions about how to remember to stop and note the proportion of engaged time. Suggest that students use the timers on their digital watches, or kitchen timers, if they have them. Notes taped to the wall or computer screen, a card placed at the top of each page as they write or read, or even the number "15" written on the back of the hand in erasable ink are all simple, effective, and unobtrusive reminders.

4. Provide students with a simple one-page form on which they can report estimated and observed totals and subtotals, as well as brief assessments of what they've learned from the exercise.

■ ANALYZING THE DATA YOU COLLECT:

The simplest first step is to calculate means for the class on each of the four values: estimated total, observed total, estimated engaged, and observed engaged time. Compare those outcomes with your own estimates.

While means are informative, it's also useful to consider the range of values, how much difference there is between highest and lowest cases. By plotting the individual "cases" out on graph paper, you can quickly get a sense of the range of your students' estimated and observed time use on one assignment.

Note whether there are identifiable subgroups within the class or whether the values are evenly spread or tightly clustered.

The comments that students make are best analyzed qualitatively. Look for patterns in their responses: How many of them were surprised by what they learned? How many were displeased? How many pleased? Did some of the students comment on why their estimated and observed totals and subtotals differed? If so, what reasons did they offer? Pay attention to what students find interesting and significant as well as to what you find interesting and significant.

■ IDEAS FOR EXTENDING AND ADAPTING:
- Do this activity twice—near the beginning and after the mid-point of the course—and compare the two sets of findings.
- Forgo the estimation step of the technique and direct students to document observed time use only.
- As a follow-up to the data analysis, ask students to suggest specific ways they could more effectively use their time.
- Encourage students to compare their self-study reports with one another.

■ PROS:
- This technique illuminates time use, making it easier for students to evaluate and perhaps change their patterns.
- It encourages self-reflection on choices and commitments.
- It provides a way for a teacher to determine if a course's workload is appropriate.

■ CONS:
- Interrupting learning time to write notes may cause some students to become distracted or frustrated. The technique does take some time away from engaged learning time.
- Students' definitions of "engaged, active learning time" will vary in degree and perhaps even in kind.
- It's hard to remember to stop at predetermined intervals as you work. Students are likely to forget to make notes at times and then have difficulties reconstructing what they did.

■ CAVEATS:
- If students suspect that their time-use patterns will be ridiculed or criticized, they are not likely to give candid responses, so anonymity must be built in to protect individuals and encourage honest reporting. The best procedure is to *require* students to turn in reports with no names on them to a secretary or teaching fellow who can check off their names on a class list.
- No matter how dismayed you may be at the results, don't berate students with them. It is much more effective to first report the results and then elicit their comments before you give any of your own.
- Warn students that it is very difficult to estimate time use and that they shouldn't be surprised if estimated and documented figures are different.

NOTES

PUNCTUATED LECTURES: LISTEN, STOP, REFLECT, WRITE, AND GIVE FEEDBACK

EASE-OF-USE RATING: III

■ DESCRIPTION:

The subtitle of this technique lists the five steps students and teachers go through in using it. Students begin by listening to a lecture or demonstration. Then, after a portion of the presentation has been completed, the teacher stops the action. For a few quiet moments, the students reflect on what they were doing during the presentation and how their behavior while listening may have helped or hindered their understanding of that information. They then write down any insights they have gained and "feed those back" to the teacher in the form of written notes or spoken comments.

■ PURPOSE:

The Punctuated Lecture technique is designed to provide immediate, on-the-spot feedback on how students are learning from a lecture or demonstration. It does this by focusing students' attention on *how* they are processing, or failing to process, the information being presented and on *how* their behavior is influencing that processing. The goal of these efforts is to help students become self-monitoring listeners and, therefore, more aware learners.

■ SUGGESTIONS FOR USE:

As the title suggests, the Punctuated Lecture technique is designed for use in classes where lectures or lecture-demonstrations are a primary method of instruction. The technique is particularly valuable when applied to lectures designed to introduce new concepts or approaches to the class.

■ EXAMPLE

After having given a basic definition and description of Classroom Research, the instructor in a teacher education course stops and asks students to reflect on what they were doing during the previous ten minutes while she was talking. She directs them to quickly recall and reconstruct a mental history of their behaviors—both mental and physical—during that period.

She gives them two minutes in which to recall their behaviors, then asks them to reflect on how those behaviors may have helped or hindered their understanding and learning of the information presented. To make this large question easier to grasp, she asks the students to consider these specific subquestions:

1. How fully and consistently were you concentrating on the lecture during those few minutes? Did you get distracted at any point? If so, how did you bring your attention back into focus?
2. What were you doing to record the information you were receiving? How successful were you?
3. What were you doing to make connections between this "new" information and what you already know?
4. What did you expect to come next in the lecture and why?

After another minute or two of silence, she directs the students each to write brief answers to each of the questions above, describing *how* they were processing the lecture and assessing *how well* their strategies were working. She allows a few minutes for students to write but does not collect their responses.

PUNCTUATED LECTURES: LISTEN, STOP, REFLECT, WRITE, AND GIVE FEEDBACK

She stops again after about twenty minutes of lecturing and quickly runs through the five steps of the technique, this time collecting their written self-assessments.

■ PROCEDURE:
1. Choose a lecture that introduces new material and that can be effectively broken up into ten- or twenty-minute segments. Decide in advance on the two spots where you will "punctuate" the lecture and schedule enough time during the session to work through the technique.
2. Don't forewarn students about the first "punctuation," but once you do stop, explain that the point is to give them an opportunity to reflect on their own learning behaviors.
3. Direct the students to take the two next steps in the process; that is, to reflect and write. Set time limits for each. Give them two to three minutes to reflect and approximately the same amount of time to write.
4. After the first run-through, collect the written feedback.

■ ANALYZING THE DATA YOU COLLECT:
Analyze the students' comments with the goal of helping them develop their skills at actively and effectively monitoring their own listening. Look at what students say they do and how they think that affects their processing. But look also at how specific and precise the language is that students use to describe what they are doing and thinking. Look for points in the listening process where you can help them by directing their attention, suggesting strategies, or simply by stopping to let the students reflect.

■ IDEAS FOR EXTENDING AND ADAPTING:
• Go through the exercise two or three times in as many weeks, stopping after progressively longer segments of the lectures.
• Ask students to save their written reflections in folders. After they've gone through the exercise a few times, direct them to analyze their responses, looking carefully for patterns and changes over time.
• Share particularly acute and detailed student reflections with the whole class as examples of effective self-analysis.
• Direct students to develop "processing plans" and to try them out in your class. In other words, once students have realized that they actually are *doing things* while they are listening and that they can choose to engage in behaviors that will be more supportive of learning, encourage them to experiment at modifying their listening behaviors in an effort to improve their learning.

■ PROS:
• Punctuated Lectures allow students and teachers to assess the information-processing behavior students engage in while listening to a lecture. In other words, it provides a window on how students learn.
• This technique promotes active listening and self-reflective learning skills that are transferable to many contexts.
• It focuses attention squarely on self-monitoring, an important component of metacognition.

■ **CONS:**
- At first many students will find it very difficult to recall and explain what they do while they are listening to a lecture and thus may find the exercise initially frustrating.
- Very few students or teachers have developed a precise and flexible vocabulary for talking about *how* they learn or about what behaviors they are engaging in as they learn. It will take time for a class to build up a meaningful, shared vocabulary with which to consider these issues.

■ **CAVEATS:**
- Don't expect immediate results from the technique. Trying to get an idea of how students process information while they are listening is a very challenging task.
- Since many people still consider the mind to be a sort of "black box," be prepared to face skepticism and a certain amount of resistance to the suggestion that explicit control over one's information processing is possible, or, if possible, a good thing.

■ **REFERENCES AND RESOURCES:**
We owe the idea for this technique to John Boehrer, Associate Director of the Harvard-Danforth Center for Teaching and Learning.

NOTES

NOTES

EASE-OF-USE RATING: IV

■ **DESCRIPTION:**
While Self-Studies of Engaged Learning Time (Technique 19) focus on how much *time* students spend in doing academic work, this technique focuses students' attention on the *process*—on *how* they do their academic work. Process Self-Analysis requires that students keep records of the actual steps they take in carrying out a representative assignment and asks them to comment on the conclusions they draw about their approaches to that assignment.

■ **PURPOSE:**
This technique gives students and teachers explicit, detailed information on the processes in which students engage as they carry out a representative assignment. This information can be used to help students pinpoint problems in their work processes and, ultimately, improve them.

■ **SUGGESTIONS FOR USE:**
This is an especially useful technique for courses in which students carry out the same type of assignment more than once during the term. Assignments in which students can do Process Self-Analyses include term papers, essays, lab reports, problem sets, and projects.

■ **EXAMPLE:**
An instructor in a developmental writing course wants to know if her students were explicitly or implicitly using "prewriting" strategies such as "free writing," "self-questioning," and "brainstorming" and if they were writing more than one draft of their weekly assignments. To find out what and how they were approaching the *process* of writing before she committed class time to teaching various approaches to the writing process, she required her students to do a Process Self-Analysis on their next weekly essay. She asked them to keep a simple record of the steps they took in preparing the essay and the approximate amount of time they dedicated to each step. She also directed them to comment briefly on how useful and helpful each step was in terms of getting the assignment done well.

■ **PROCEDURE:**
1. Choose an assignment that meets the following three criteria:
   a. You are interested in how students work through it.
   b. Your students are quite likely to benefit from focusing on it and will get another chance to use what they've learned.
   c. The assignment is complex enough to provide an interesting process analysis.
2. Let students know from the outset, before you give the focus assignment itself, that they will be required to keep a record of their work processes— what steps they took, how much time each took—and write that up as an assessment technique.
3. Give instructions and examples of how to keep records of their processes, what to include, and how long the final product should be.
4. Ask students to hand the Process Self-Analysis in with or immediately after handing in the assignment itself.

■ **ANALYZING THE DATA YOU COLLECT:**
Read and grade the assignments themselves first—without looking at the Process Self-Analyses. Then, read the Process Self-Analyses and assess the overall work schemes for clarity and explicitness, the number of steps taken, the effectiveness of each step, overall time devoted to the assignment, time devoted to each step, and so on. Look for similarities and differences among students' analyses in number, content, and order of the steps. See if there are any clear patterns most students share.

■ **IDEAS FOR EXTENDING AND ADAPTING:**
• Stagger the Process Self-Analysis exercise so that only a few students are doing it at any given time. This makes assessment less burdensome.
• Have students read each others' Process Self-Analyses and compare notes on how they proceeded.
• Direct students to focus on only one stage of the process, such as the beginning or the end.
• Ask students to focus on one element of the process that they would like to change and to explicitly redesign their processes to accomplish that change.

■ **PROS:**
• Process Analysis focuses student and teacher attention on the most transferable elements of the lesson by focusing on process rather than on products.
• By explicitly breaking down the work process into distinct steps, Process Self-Analysis allows students and teachers to tinker with and improve those steps and, consequently, to make the whole process more effective.
• It lets teachers see *how much* time the students spend on assignments and *how* they spend that time.
• Process analysis allows teachers to compare the steps the students actually go through in completing an assignment with the steps the teacher of the course thinks they should go through.
• This technique may help uncover generally productive strategies. These productive strategies can be shared among the students and incorporated into the teachers' repertoires.

■ **CONS:**
• Students may resist keeping a process record, or even if they are willing, find it time consuming and difficult.
• Teachers may discover that their evaluations of the quality of students' assignments are not highly correlated with the amount of time and sincere effort the students devote to them.

■ **CAVEATS:**
• Don't make this assessment technique so complex and demanding that it overwhelms the assignment it is based on. Ask students to outline the process they've gone through, not to narrate it.
• Those students who could most benefit from analyzing their own work may be the least motivated to do so. Consider offering a reward for the quite difficult

work involved in working through this technique. That reward might be a small, fixed number of points added to the assignment grade for those who complete the analysis.

NOTES

3. Write a few questions that you need answers to before you can understand the points listed in ?.

II. Homework Assignment/Test Entry

1. Briefly describe the assignment/test: What was it about?

2. Give one or two examples of your most successful responses. Try to explain what critical things you did that made them successful.

3. Give one or two examples, if relevant, of errors or less successful responses. What did you do wrong or fail to do in each case?

4. Comment briefly to remind yourself what to be sure to do the next time you confront a similar situation and what you should do differently to increase your learning.

■ PROCEDURE:

1. Let students know that you will be asking them to keep records of their learning in the form of class notes, assignments, tests, and quizzes. Explain also that they will be assessing their own learning, their successes, and their failures. Tell them why you are asking them to do this, explaining the benefits both you and they should derive from the technique.

2. Provide them with a sample format, such as the one used in the example above. Work through the technique in class, modeling and explaining as necessary.

3. Help students focus by pointing out strengths and weaknesses, successes and failures, correct responses and errors in their work. Be selective, however, and limit your comments to a few important points.

4. Ask students to make copies of their logs and hand in those copies at set intervals. Your first deadline should be after one or two weeks, just to check whether students understand the process. After you're sure they get it, you might ask for submissions monthly or at natural breaks in the course schedule.

■ ANALYZING THE DATA YOU COLLECT:

The main point of assessing these logs is to compare the teacher's sense of what the class is and isn't understanding and why with the students' self-reports and self-analyses. Assess the logs to discover the range and kind of responses students make to their own learning by keeping a record of the kinds of questions students raise and the types of problems they identify.

One simple way to categorize responses follows: (0) Doesn't identify successful or unsuccessful responses; (1) identifies but doesn't diagnose causes of successful or unsuccessful responses; (2) identifies and diagnoses, but doesn't offer solutions; or, (3) identifies, diagnoses, and offers solutions.

As you repeat this technique, you will also be able to assess what impact the steps you have taken in response to the students' logs have had. Repeat analyses will show if there are changes in students' skills at identifying, diagnosing, and prescribing solutions to their own learning problems.

■ IDEAS FOR EXTENDING AND ADAPTING:

- Read and assess logs from a different subgroup of students each week as a way of spreading out the work.
- Give students explicit guidelines as to the types of information on which to focus their log entries.
- Limit the amount of data you collect by including fewer questions in your format or by asking students to indicate those sections of their logs they want you to assess.

■ PROS:

- Self-diagnostic learning logs encourage students to become more self-reflective, active, and independent learners.
- The technique introduces students to a self-assessment protocol that can be transferred to virtually any learning situation.
- It provides the teacher with organized, classifiable, and assessable data on students' metacognitive skills, their skills at observing, evaluating, and criticizing their own learning.
- The learning logs can provide teachers with valuable insights and suggestions from the students for improving learning.

■ CONS:

- Learning logs are essentially another ongoing assignment that requires time and effort from students and teachers.
- Unless a continuing attempt is made to focus on strengths and successes, this technique can leave students demoralized from paying too much attention to their weaknesses and failures.

■ CAVEATS:

- Chances are good that most students will have had little previous experience at structured self-assessment. Don't give up if their first efforts show weak self-critical skills. Instead, teach them, through coaching and illustration, how to carry out the technique.
- Resist the temptation to focus only on what the students don't understand and can't do. Try to give almost as much attention to skills and knowledge they can build on in positive ways. Encourage them to capitalize on their strengths as they improve their weaknesses.
- Don't try to read too many at any one time, and don't feel bound to read every word.

3. Write a few questions that you need answers to before you can understand the points listed in 2.

II. Homework Assignment/Test Entry

1. Briefly describe the assignment/test: What was it about?

2. Give one or two examples of your most successful responses. Try to explain what critical things you did that made them successful.

3. Give one or two examples, if relevant, of errors or less successful responses. What did you do wrong or fail to do in each case?

4. Comment briefly to remind yourself what to be sure to do the next time you confront a similar situation and what you should do differently to increase your learning.

■ **PROCEDURE:**
1. Let students know that you will be asking them to keep records of their learning in the form of class notes, assignments, tests, and quizzes. Explain also that they will be assessing their own learning, their successes, and their failures. Tell them why you are asking them to do this, explaining the benefits both you and they should derive from the technique.
2. Provide them with a sample format, such as the one used in the example above. Work through the technique in class, modeling and explaining as necessary.
3. Help students focus by pointing out strengths and weaknesses, successes and failures, correct responses and errors in their work. Be selective, however, and limit your comments to a few important points.
4. Ask students to make copies of their logs and hand in those copies at set intervals. Your first deadline should be after one or two weeks, just to check whether students understand the process. After you're sure they get it, you might ask for submissions monthly or at natural breaks in the course schedule.

■ **ANALYZING THE DATA YOU COLLECT:**
The main point of assessing these logs is to compare the teacher's sense of what the class is and isn't understanding and why with the students' self-reports and self-analyses. Assess the logs to discover the range and kind of responses students make to their own learning by keeping a record of the kinds of questions students raise and the types of problems they identify.

One simple way to categorize responses follows: (0) Doesn't identify successful or unsuccessful responses; (1) identifies but doesn't diagnose causes of successful or unsuccessful responses; (2) identifies and diagnoses, but doesn't offer solutions; or, (3) identifies, diagnoses, and offers solutions.

As you repeat this technique, you will also be able to assess what impact the steps you have taken in response to the students' logs have had. Repeat analyses will show if there are changes in students' skills at identifying, diagnosing, and prescribing solutions to their own learning problems.

■ IDEAS FOR EXTENDING AND ADAPTING:
- Read and assess logs from a different subgroup of students each week as a way of spreading out the work.
- Give students explicit guidelines as to the types of information on which to focus their log entries.
- Limit the amount of data you collect by including fewer questions in your format or by asking students to indicate those sections of their logs they want you to assess.

■ PROS:
- Self-diagnostic learning logs encourage students to become more self-reflective, active, and independent learners.
- The technique introduces students to a self-assessment protocol that can be transferred to virtually any learning situation.
- It provides the teacher with organized, classifiable, and assessable data on students' metacognitive skills, their skills at observing, evaluating, and criticizing their own learning.
- The learning logs can provide teachers with valuable insights and suggestions from the students for improving learning.

■ CONS:
- Learning logs are essentially another ongoing assignment that requires time and effort from students and teachers.
- Unless a continuing attempt is made to focus on strengths and successes, this technique can leave students demoralized from paying too much attention to their weaknesses and failures.

■ CAVEATS:
- Chances are good that most students will have had little previous experience at structured self-assessment. Don't give up if their first efforts show weak self-critical skills. Instead, teach them, through coaching and illustration, how to carry out the technique.
- Resist the temptation to focus only on what the students don't understand and can't do. Try to give almost as much attention to skills and knowledge they can build on in positive ways. Encourage them to capitalize on their strengths as they improve their weaknesses.
- Don't try to read too many at any one time, and don't feel bound to read every word.

■ **REFERENCES AND RESOURCES:**
In the last decade, much has been written about the uses of journal writing as a learning tool, particularly, though not exclusively, by composition teachers. Selfe and Arbabi (1986) and Selfe, Petersen, and Nahrgang (1986) describe experiments in focused academic journal writing in engineering and mathematics courses, respectively. Both of these articles are contained in Young and Fulwiler (1986).

NOTES

they labeled as follows: "skill," which represents the ability to communicate in an interesting way, to stimulate intellectual curiosity, and to explain clearly; "rapport," which involves empathy, interaction with and concern for students; "structure," which concerns organization and presentation of course material; and "overload," which refers to the workload and instructor demands.

While the research gives some confidence that good teachers have certain characteristics in common, and that these can be reliably identified by students, the research on the *usefulness* of these evaluations to teachers is less optimistic. Student evaluations of teachers and courses have become well-accepted by faculty members and are now used on most college campuses for evaluation purposes (Seldin, 1984), but there is, as yet, little evidence that teachers change their behaviors as a result of such feedback (Centra, 1973; Blackburn et al., 1986). This may be, in part, the result of the lack of involvement of individual teachers in the design of the evaluation measures and, in part, the result of widespread failure to design student evaluations to explicitly help teachers improve their teaching.

Riegle and Rhodes (1986) point out that most faculty evaluation procedures have multiple purposes—to appoint, to tenure, to inform salary and promotion decisions, to terminate, and to help teachers improve. It is the last purpose that interests us here, and in that context Riegle and Rhodes suggest that the metaphor of "critiquing" is more appropriate than the usual metaphors of rating, assessing, appraising, or judging. If evaluations encouraged students to "critique" rather than "judge" teaching and course material, the results might be more useful.

We believe that it is possible to effect significant improvement in teaching through obtaining feedback from students, especially—perhaps only—if individual teachers are able to design the types of feedback that will be most useful and most acceptable to them. The purpose of the assessment suggestions given in the sections on teaching methods and on course materials is to help teachers think about new ways to collect data that shed light on the questions they have about their own teaching and about the course organization and materials they are using.

Assessing Student Reactions to Teachers and Teaching Methods

Many departments, programs and colleges use teacher evaluation forms—whether in-house or commercial products—as a source of information for tenuring, reappointing, and promoting faculty members. However, few such evaluations are designed to directly improve teaching and learning in the classrooms of those same faculty members. Even when the results are shared with the teachers who've been evaluated, it's often very difficult for them to draw useful conclusions from such instruments about how to improve their teaching.

Three of the four techniques in this subsection are designed to provide context- and teacher-specific feedback that can be translated into improved teaching. They all emphasize the important role students have to play as observers and assessors of teaching while providing ways to improve students' skills at constructively carrying out those roles.

The three differ primarily in level of complexity and ease of use. While Student-Teacher Electronic Mail Messages make very limited demands on the students, this technique requires that teachers define and pose questions about their teaching in ways that students can answer constructively in a brief letter format through electronic mail. Chain Notes provide the teacher with information on what students are thinking while the class is in progress—immediate, spontaneous reactions rather than post hoc, considered reflections. Teacher-Designed Evaluation Mini-Forms combine the ease of administration and analysis inherent in traditional, structured teacher evaluation questionnaires with the course-specific, action-oriented focus of the classroom teacher.

The final technique in this subsection aims at covering students' images of good teachers. Through their students' Profiles of Admirable Teachers, teachers can learn what their students value in teaching and thus get a glimpse into the implicit and explicit criteria and expectations their students bring to their assessments of teachers.

EASE-OF-USE RATING: I

■ DESCRIPTION:

This is one of the simplest techniques possible for eliciting and assessing students' reactions to teachers in courses making use of computer. The teacher writes an open letter to the class via electronic mail, raising a few questions about his or her teaching and inviting student responses. That open letter asks students to respond to the teacher's questions in the form of a personal, though anonymous, message sent to the teacher's electronic mailbox.

■ PURPOSE:

The purpose of Student-Teacher Electronic Mail Messages is to provide a simple and familiar format through which teachers can ask and students can respond to questions about the teacher's performance. The reason for using the electronic mail message format is that it encourages personal, informal, and open-ended responses to questions teachers pose.

■ SUGGESTIONS FOR USE:

This technique is useful whenever the teacher feels there may be a problem in the class that hasn't surfaced, before or after high-stress periods such as exams or holidays, or at pre-set intervals.

■ EXAMPLE:

The following is an example of an open letter from a teacher to his students via electronic mail:

Dear Students,

Overall, I've been very pleased with our class and feel things are going well. I'm convinced, though, that there's always room for improvement, so I'd like to get your responses to a couple of questions about ways my teaching may affect your learning.

Can you think of examples of things that I do or say—my teaching behaviors—that make it easier or more interesting to learn in my class? How about things that I do or say that make it harder or less interesting?

What advice can you give me that might make me a better teacher for you?

Please write me a short mail message responding to my questions. Be as specific, informative, honest, and constructive as you can in your responses. So that you'll feel totally free to respond frankly, I'd like these letters to be anonymous—don't put your user name on them.

I'd like to receive these messages before the next class session. I'll read them with sincere interest and seriously consider your suggestions. After I've read them, I'll write another message to the class summarizing your responses and letting you know what I plan to do about your ideas.

Classroom Assessment Technique 23
STUDENT-TEACHER ELECTRONIC MAIL MESSAGES

■ PROCEDURE:
1. Determine one or two questions about your teaching to which you'd like to know students' reactions. Make sure these are questions about teaching behaviors you can—and may be willing to—change. One criterion for a good question to ask is this: Are students likely to have ideas and opinions about this topic that will help me improve my teaching?
2. Write a friendly and informal open letter to the class. Tell them what you want to know and why. Send it to their electronic mailboxes or to an electronic class bulletin board.
3. Give students clear instructions on when and how to respond to your message.

■ ANALYZING THE DATA YOU COLLECT:
The analysis of these electronic mail messages ought to be quite straight-forward. Note and summarize answers to your questions and categorize them into types or themes if possible. Keep a record also of concerns and comments that surface in the letters that *aren't* direct responses to your questions. These may represent important and highly charged feelings and opinions about your teaching.

■ IDEAS FOR EXTENDING AND ADAPTING:
• Ask the students to write the letters as though they were writing to a third party of their choice about your teaching. This may help them be less inhibited.
• If you can avail yourself of a trusted peer or faculty development consultant, have the students actually write about you to that person. Ask your peer or consultant to summarize the contents and report them to you. This is another way to encourage honesty and openness.
• If you don't have easy access to computers or electronic mail, do this technique with real letters. Make sure to find ways to safeguard student anonymity.

■ PROS:
• The letter format allows for a large range of diversity in content, tone, and length of response.
• The technique can be used to familiarize students with the use of electronic mail, a valuable skill.
• Letters are a kind of writing most students are familiar with, and some are letter writers in their personal lives.
• This technique encourages direct, personal, and candid responses.

■ CONS:
• The wide range of responses you receive may be rather difficult to categorize.
• You may receive more suggestions than you want or can handle.
• The comments you receive may be more critical than you expect.
• Using this technique implies that you will do something in response to students' opinions. If you fail to respond, you may lose student respect and trust.

• Some students may feel reluctant to criticize or feel that their writing styles will reveal their identity.

■ **CAVEATS:**
• Don't ask questions about areas of your teaching you can't or won't change.
• Try to distinguish comments about the course from comments about your teaching.
• Stress the importance of anonymity, but provide other channels for those students who want to respond directly and individually. Appointments are a good means for assessing individual reactions.

■ **REFERENCES AND RESOURCES:**
Although some of its technical details are out of date, Heinz Dreher's (1984) article provides a simple and clear argument for the use of electronic mail in the classroom.

NOTES

NOTES

■ **DESCRIPTION:**

In this technique, students in a lecture course pass around a large envelope on which the teacher has written a question about the class. The students have all been given index cards at the beginning of class. When the envelope reaches a student, he or she spends one or two minutes writing a response to the question and then drops the card in the envelope and passes it on. This technique results in a rich, composite record of each individual student's reactions to the class in action. In this way, Chain Notes allow teachers a view of their classes through their students' eyes.

■ **PURPOSE:**

The purpose of Chain Notes is to elicit very limited written feedback from each student in a class about what he or she is thinking or noticing about the teaching and learning occurring at a given moment in the class session. This feedback can give the teacher a "sounding" of the students' level of engagement and involvement as well as tell the teacher what the students are really attending to during the course of the class. This kind of feedback provides information data on students' reactions to the teaching.

■ **SUGGESTIONS FOR USE:**

Chain Notes make the most sense in large lecture or lecture-discussion classes where students have little direct contact with the teacher. The focus of the Chain Note can be virtually open-ended or rather specific, depending on the directions the students receive. In general, the more specific the prompt, the more useful and informative the comments.

■ **EXAMPLE:**

To assess how students were reacting to the lectures in his large Introduction to Psychology course, the instructor decided to make use of the Chain Notes technique. He wrote across the front of a large manila envelope: "How clear is the content and purpose of the lecture to you at this moment?" He handed out 3-by-5 index cards at the beginning of the following class and directed the students to respond to the question on the envelope in one or two minutes, drop their cards in the envelope, then pass it on.

■ **ANALYZING THE DATA YOU COLLECT:**

You can make a first cut at the data by categorizing reactions in any of the following ways: engaged/not engaged; focus on self/focus on teacher/focus on students/focus on content; question/praise/neutral comment/complaint; or, on-target/off-target/can't tell.

Whatever criteria you use for analyzing the data, the point should be to detect reactions that provide clues about how to improve the class from the students' perspectives.

■ **IDEAS FOR EXTENDING AND ADAPTING:**

• Make a videotape or audiotape recording of the class in which students are writing Chain Notes. Before you read the students' reactions to the live class, play the recording and write your own Chain Notes in reaction to that video. Then, compare your notes to the students' and see if you can guess the approximate times the notes were written. Try to identify the stimuli that prompted student reactions.

- Use Chain Notes two or three times over the course of four to six weeks and note any changes you observe in the sophistication, content, and tone of the notes.

■ PROS:

- The Chain Notes technique elicits feedback from every member of the class.
- It encourages students to be reflective, evaluative, and active observers and requires that they monitor what they are taking in.
- The responses tend to be very spontaneous and honest, due both to the nature of the task and the guarantee of anonymity.
- The reactions are more concrete and specific than those students give in end-of-term evaluations. The technique generates a collage of "snapshots" of the class dynamic.
- It helps the teacher to spot positive and negative trends in the class. This early-warning device can help teachers build on the former and ameliorate the latter.

■ CONS:

- The act of writing down the note can distract the student from whatever is going on in the class at that moment. Some students resent being asked to divide their attention.
- By their very nature, Chain Notes are episodic and fragmentary, and so may be difficult to interpret.
- Some students, particularly those in small classes, may hesitate to respond honestly for fear that the teacher will recognize their handwriting.
- Other students may focus on "unalterable" variables—those elements of the classroom environment we cannot change, such as an instructor's slight but unfortunate resemblance to a murderer in a play!

■ CAVEATS:

- This is not a device for the thin-skinned, nor for those teachers who are convinced that they command their students' absolute attention.
- Remember that the parts of a Chain Note don't necessarily sum up to any coherent whole. Rather they give suggestive insights.
- It's unwise to base major changes in a course or in your teaching on the reactions in one Chain Note. While this is a good exploratory technique, it is not a valid confirmatory one. Follow up on ideas suggested by the technique by using other, more focused, and less hurried assessment techniques.

NOTES

NOTES

■ **DESCRIPTION:**

One reason teacher evaluation forms are so widely used is that they package student assessments of teachers in a form that is easily administered, coded, and analyzed. In addition, the information from various administrations of the same evaluation form can be easily compared. By using this technique, teachers can benefit from the advantages of evaluation forms and collect information on questions they consider critical to improving their teaching by preparing simple, short, course-specific evaluation mini-forms. These mini-forms contain three to five questions, all to be answered either with scale-o-grams, multiple-choice answers or short fill-in answers.

■ **PURPOSE:**

Teacher-Designed Evaluation Mini-Forms collect limited, focused data on student reactions to questions the teacher considers important in a form that is easily quantified and compared.

■ **SUGGESTIONS FOR USE:**

To get information early enough to make changes and to measure progress over time, administer Teacher-Designed Evaluation Mini-Forms at regular intervals, such as one-third and two-thirds or one-quarter, one-half, and three-quarters of the way through the course. If your purpose is to gather information about a specific problem or question, however, you may want to prepare and administer Mini-Forms at other times. The best time to administer these forms is during the last 10 to 15 minutes of the class and, if possible, during the last meeting of the week. This will avoid derailing other learning activities and will allow you time to analyze the responses before the next class session.

■ **EXAMPLE:**

The following is a sample teacher evaluation mini-form that one of the authors has developed and used in several undergraduate and graduate courses. The purpose of these particular questions is to measure the degree to which the instructor is meeting three of his most important goals for the course: fair and equal treatment of students, efficient use of class time, and useful response to student learning.

```
Directions: Please respond honestly and constructively to
            the questions below by circling the responses
            you most agree with and writing comments to
            explain them.  I ask these questions to find
            out how I'm doing and to get ideas from you
            on how to improve my effectiveness.

1. From your perspective, how successful am I at treating
   all the students in the class with fairness and
   respect?

   Total Failure    0  1  2  3  4  5    Total Success

   Comments on specific ways I might improve? _____
```

2. How efficiently do I organize and use class time to promote student learning?

   Totally Inefficient 0 1 2 3 4 5 Totally Efficient

   Comments on specific ways I could teach more efficiently?

   _____

   _____

3. How helpful are my comments on your papers and responses to your written questions in helping you understand the course material?

   Not At All Helpful 0 1 2 3 4 5 Always Very Helpful

   Any suggestions on how I could make my comments and responses more helpful?_____

   _____

■ PROCEDURE:
1. Write up three to five specific questions about your teaching that you'd like students to respond to. Make sure that those questions relate directly to your instructional goals for the class.
2. Develop appropriate coded responses, either multiple choice or scales, for those questions.
3. Make up a one-page, carefully worded form to collect focused and constructive responses.
4. To protect anonymity, have students turn in forms to a teaching fellow or secretary or leave them in an envelope pinned to your office door.

■ ANALYZING THE DATA YOU COLLECT
In analyzing student responses to these Mini-Forms, it is both methodologically sound and pedagogically useful to give more attention to the direction, intensity, and consistency of the responses than to their actual numerical values or means. The pre-coded responses make it easy to see patterns in the responses across the whole class. For example, if you simply tally the number of students who circled 0, 1, 2, 3 and so on for each question, you can quickly see areas of disagreement, agreement, or polarization within the class. The comments, though less easily compared, often provide teachers with the most useful feedback for improving their teaching.

■ IDEAS FOR EXTENDING AND ADAPTING:
• After you've gone through this process once, ask students to come up with questions they'd like to see on the next Mini-Form. They can devise these questions individually, or produce them as the result of a structured group exercise.
• After you've analyzed the Mini-Forms, summarize the results to the class and outline the specific action(s) you intend to take in response to student reactions.

■ **PROS:**
- By explicitly assessing your teaching to find out how well you are achieving your instructional goals, you publicly demonstrate your commitment to those goals, your respect for students' assessments, and your professional integrity.
- If you construct the questions carefully, the students' responses should provide the kind of context-specific, focused feedback you need to make adjustments in your teaching.
- In carrying out this technique and following up with related adjustments, you provide a role model for students of a professional who is sufficiently self-assured to listen to and learn from his or her students' criticisms, opinions, and insights.

Teaching students, *by personal example,* the value of inviting and welcoming evaluation by others is one of the most important outcomes of this technique. Since evaluation is a constant in student life and a critical factor in many jobs, students who learn to make constructive use of it—rather than fearing or resenting the process—will gain distinct advantages.

■ **CONS:**
- Because of their own fear of criticism or dislike of evaluation, some students may view your use of the Mini-Forms as an admission that something is wrong or as a sign of weakness.
- Good Mini-Forms take a lot of thought to construct. Once you have a useful one, though, you may be able to use it in other, similar courses.
- You may receive responses you feel do not respond to the questions or do not respond to them constructively.

■ **CAVEATS:**
- Anonymity is a necessary precondition to honest assessment.
- Ask questions about alterable variables, those elements of your teaching behavior you can and are willing to change.
- Don't promise any changes that you may not be able to deliver, and always promise somewhat less than you are confident you can achieve. It's generally a good tactic to risk exceeding your predictions by making modest promises rather than failing to achieve ambitious ones.
- Don't overuse the Mini-Form technique. Two or perhaps three administrations over the course of a semester will indicate change without risking overkill.

NOTES

EASE-OF-USE RATING: IV

■ DESCRIPTION:

This straightforward technique requires that students write a brief, focused profile of a teacher whose values, skills, and actions they greatly admire.

■ PURPOSE:

This technique elicits information about what students value in their teachers in a very concrete way by asking them two things: (1) to select and profile a teacher whose values and behavior they admire; and (2) to explain what they find admirable and why. This information can help teachers understand the images and criteria students bring to their evaluation.

■ SUGGESTIONS FOR USE:

This technique is useful for courses in which students are expected to explore their values in systematic ways. It can help students recognize their values in relation to a given job or profession and make them explicit. It is best used early in the term, before students are asked to systematically analyze their values, which provides baseline information on students' values and their level of sophistication in expressing them.

■ EXAMPLE:

The teacher of a course titled Ethics in Business wants to know whom her students consider as role models of ethical businesspeople. She also wants to collect information on what characteristics the students particularly value in teachers of ethics in business, whether those teachers are professional classroom teachers or model businesspeople who teach by example.

To elicit such information, she asks each student to prepare a profile of a businessperson whom they consider particularly admirable—both as an ethical model and as a teacher. The directions are reproduced below:

```
                  Profile of an Admirable Teacher

Directions:   Select a businessperson whom you view as a
              model of ethical behavior—an admirable
              practitioner—and as a model teacher.  Write
              a two- or three-page profile of that person,
              focusing on examples of the qualities that
              make that person admirable in both roles.
              In other words, show rather than tell why
              this person is a role model.  Then, explain
              what the qualities are that you find most
              appealing in this person.
```

■ PROCEDURE:

1. Begin by trying the technique yourself:
   Can you think of one or more truly admirable teachers in your field? Can you explain and give examples of how and why each person you've selected was an admirable teacher?

2. If you *can* think of a few admirable teachers and are confident that your students can as well, decide what criteria you will use in assessing their profiles. Those criteria should focus on such qualities as clarity, completeness, and persuasiveness of the profiles rather than on the identity of the teachers chosen as the subjects.

3. Draw up clear directions for the profiles and hand them out.

■ **ANALYZING THE DATA YOU COLLECT:**
The most useful data these profiles can yield is on the qualities and characteristics of the teachers that students choose: what students identify as admirable. In a very real sense, while the identities of those profiled are relatively unimportant, the identities of the values they represent to the students are critical. Therefore, one easy way to analyze the results is to tally the times that particular characteristics or values—such as honesty, hard work, respect for students, enthusiasm, and love of learning—are mentioned in the profiles. This can provide a kind of straw poll of the values students in your class most admire.

■ **IDEAS FOR EXTENDING AND ADAPTING:**
• Provide students with a list of possible subjects: teachers who are widely regarded as admirable, and about whom the students can write profiles if they don't have candidates of their own.
• Ask students to write parallel profiles of teachers who are distinctly not admirable. Request that they not name names.
• Direct students to reread their profiles and to list, in rank order of importance, the characteristics and values their subjects embodied.
• Have students work in small groups, with each member reading the profiles written by others. Ask each group to draw up a composite profile of an admirable teacher.

■ **PROS:**
• Writing a profile of an admirable teacher requires the student to consider his or her own values and to make choices that are based on that valuing.
• This technique provides teachers with clear information on the students' images of admirable teachers. Since such images often serve as guides and goals during adolescence and early adulthood, explicitly knowing the key qualities of these role models is critical to teachers and to students alike.

■ **CONS:**
• Locating the information on characteristics in these profiles is often a challenge. It requires close reading and, sometimes, reading between the lines. The less explicit students are, the more time teachers spend reading.

■ **CAVEATS:**
• Many students may be unable, at least at first, to come up with teachers to profile. Or they may limit their profiles to telling the life stories of the individuals rather than focusing explicitly on their characteristics as teachers. Those

students will need explicit guidelines and may need instruction in how to write well-focused profiles.
- Some students may choose to write about teachers whom you find personally unadmirable, or about whom you have no knowledge. In both cases, keep in mind that the identity of the subject is much less important than the description and illustration of the qualities and characteristics the chosen teacher embodies.

NOTES

NOTES

Assessing Student Reactions to Course Materials, Activities, and Assignments

While the four techniques in the previous subsection focused on student reactions to teaching and teachers, the techniques in this subsection focus on student reactions to the assignments, materials, and activities that make up a particular course. One-Minute Papers is the most open-ended and flexible of the techniques and can be used to elicit student reactions to virtually any simple questions. The RSQC2 technique is much more structured and sequential and focuses clearly on student recall, reaction, and evaluation of classroom activities. The Exam Evaluation technique is the most specialized and limited in scope of the four in this subsection, dealing as it does with one type of assignment. Given the almost universal use of tests and exams, however, this technique should find application in a great many classrooms. Classroom Assessment Quality Circles, on the other hand, an idea adapted from the use of Quality Circles in business and industry, can be used to assess any element of courses.

EASE-OF-USE RATING: I

■ **DESCRIPTION:**
One-Minute Papers, a technique also known as the Half-Sheet Response, provide a quick and extremely simple way to collect written feedback on student reactions. The teacher stops class a few minutes early and poses one or two questions to which students are asked to react. The students write their reactions on half-sheets of paper (hence the second name), or index cards, the teacher has handed out.

■ **PURPOSE:**
One-Minute Papers elicit timely and limited student feedback on one or two specific questions about the course in general or a specific class session. That feedback will help teachers decide if midcourse corrections or changes are needed and, if so, what kinds to make.

■ **SUGGESTIONS FOR USE:**
One-Minute Papers are probably most useful in large lecture or lecture/discussion courses, although the technique can be easily adapted to other settings. The questions that teachers pose may concern class procedures, content, materials, activities and assignments, or any other specific element that the teacher wants to examine. One-Minute Papers work best at the end—or the beginning—of a class session. It is a productive warm-up or wrap-up activity.

■ **EXAMPLE:**
After the first three weeks of the semester, a chemistry teacher has the feeling that the students in her undergraduate chemistry class—a lecture and lab class with 150 students—may not be getting all that they should from her lectures. Ten minutes before the end of the class period, she quickly passes out 3-by-5 index cards to the class. She then asks them to write a very brief answer on the cards to the following two questions:

1. What was the most important thing you learned in today's class?
2. What question or questions that you have from today's class remain unanswered?

■ **PROCEDURE:**
1. Write down one or two questions about the course content, activities or materials to which you'd like your students to respond. Are they questions that the students can answer quickly and briefly? To what extent are you willing to act on the students' responses? If you decide your question is appropriate and if you are willing to respond to the One-Minute Papers, plan to set aside five to ten minutes of your next class to use the technique.
2. During the first or last few minutes of the class session, hand out index cards or ask students to take out a half-sheet of paper.
3. Unless there is a very good reason to know who wrote what, direct students to leave their names *off* the paper or card.
4. Write one or, at the most, two questions on the chalkboard and ask students to respond to them frankly and concisely—in single words, short phrases, or very short sentences, as appropriate.

5. Let the students know how much time they will have—five to ten minutes is usually enough.

■ ANALYZING THE DATA YOU COLLECT:
Simply tabulating the answers and making note of any useful comments is probably all the analysis needed.

■ IDEAS FOR EXTENDING AND ADAPTING:
• Give students a few extra minutes to compare and discuss their responses with their classmates.
• Give groups of students the opportunity to suggest questions for the One-Minute Papers and let them tabulate, analyze, and present the results to the whole class.
• Use the technique to collect quick feedback on knowledge or understanding, values and opinions, reactions to teaching, or any of the other topics mentioned in this handbook.

■ PROS:
• This technique can provide valuable self-correcting feedback that results in more effective teaching and learning.
• One-Minute Papers provide immediate midcourse feedback to teachers and allow quick response to students. This is especially important in classrooms, where so many issues have limited life spans and time is always in short supply.
• The responses—even from a very large class—can be read, tabulated, and analyzed in a short time and with limited effort.
• By demonstrating respect for and interest in student reactions, this technique encourages active engagement in the class process—something that's often lacking in large classes.
• It allows individual students to compare their responses with those of the class as a whole. Students can find out the degree to which their reactions or opinions are shared by their classmates.

■ CONS:
• If One-Minute Papers are overused or poorly used, the technique can degenerate into a gimmick or a *pro forma* exercise in polling.
• It may elicit feedback that teachers or students don't want to hear or don't want to act on.
• It's more difficult than it may seem to prepare a question that can be immediately and clearly comprehended and quickly answered.

■ CAVEATS:
• Asking students to respond to questions about your course is likely to raise expectations that you are planning to make changes. If you're not sure why you want the information you are about to collect or what you will do about it once you've got it, you're better off *not* using this technique.

■ **REFERENCES:**

The term *half-sheet response* comes from an article on this technique by Weaver and Cotrell (1985). Wilson (1986) reports the use of a very similar technique which he refers to as *Minute Papers,* and it is that article on which this technique is based. Both articles give information on applications of this technique in college classes. In addition, an upcoming issue of the Harvard University Danforth Center's journal, *Teaching and Learning,* will feature an article by Frederick Mosteller detailing his successful adaptation of this technique for use with an undergraduate statistics course.

NOTES

NOTES

RSQC2 (RECALL, SUMMARIZE, QUESTION, COMMENT, AND CONNECT)

EASE-OF-USE RATING: III

■ **DESCRIPTION:**

This five-step protocol guides students quickly through simple recall, summary, analysis, evaluation, and synthesis exercises focusing on the previous class or several previous classes.

■ **PURPOSE:**

RSQC2 allows the teacher to compare detailed information on the students' recall, understanding, and evaluation of the class against his or her own. It also informs the teacher of student questions and comments that need timely responses.

■ **SUGGESTIONS FOR USE:**

This technique is best used at regular intervals. If classes meet only once or twice a week, it can profitably be used to begin each class. If classes meet every day, or three times a week, consider using it to end—or begin and end—the week. It's not necessary to go through all of the steps in the procedure to benefit from the technique. It can be very useful to work through two or three different steps each time.

■ **EXAMPLE:**

At the beginning of the second of four workshops on Classroom Research, the presenter decided to check the participants' understanding of the first day's session. He asked the participants to work through the first four steps in the RSQC2 technique at the start of the session. Then, after about twenty minutes of the second day's presentation, he asked them to connect the first day's work with that of the second.

■ **PROCEDURE:**

1. At the beginning of the class session ask students to make a list—in words or simple phrases—of what they recall as the most important/interesting/difficult/useful points from the previous class session. This should take three to five minutes.
2. Solicit the recalled information from the class, writing summary words and phrases on the board. Make sure to invite students to add any missing points to their lists. This should take three to five minutes.
3. Ask each student to choose, from the revised list, the three to five main points of the previous lesson and rank them in order of importance. This should take two to three minutes at most.
4. Now direct the students to summarize the previous class in one sentence that includes all their main points, if possible. Give them one to two minutes to write this summary sentence.
5. Next, ask them to jot down one or two questions that remain unanswered after the previous class. Allow one or two minutes again.
6. Invite the students to write an evaluative comment or two about the class. Here are a few possible comment stems you can suggest as starting points: What I enjoyed most/least was ... What I found most/least useful was... This step also requires a couple of minutes.

RSQC2 (RECALL, SUMMARIZE, QUESTION, COMMENT, AND CONNECT)

7. Finally, ask students to state what they see as the connection(s) between the main point(s) of the previous class and the major goal(s) of the entire course. Ask them to express this in one or two sentences written in as many minutes.

8. Ask the students to turn in all or part of their responses anonymously.

■ ANALYZING THE DATA YOU COLLECT:

If you have gone through the protocol and written down your responses, you can compare them with those of your students. Note whether or not you've got the same basic points in the same ranked order. Keep track of omissions, additions, and errors in the students' responses—and your own. Look for patterns in the questions and comments: Do several students mention the same basic ones? Assess the degree of "fit" between your summary of the class and the students'. Do the same for the sentences on connections.

■ IDEAS FOR EXTENDING AND ADAPTING:

• After the process is clearly understood, let students take over the teacher's role. A different student or pair of students can be responsible for each class session.

• Let the responsible student(s) carry out steps 1 to 3, or 1 to 4, before class and share their results, saving class time.

■ PROS:

• RSQC2 gives the teacher immediate feedback on what students noticed/learned/remembered/(mis-)understood/valued from the previous class.

• It gives students a highly structured opportunity to explicitly recall, summarize, and evaluate material presented in a previous class and to compare or share their recall, understanding, and evaluation with fellow students and the teacher.

• It helps build a shared conception of course goals, objectives, content, and direction among all participants.

• By stressing connections, it provides an explicit "bridge" from "old" to "new" information and ideas.

• RSQC2 forces participants to continually review, recycle, reorganize, reconsider, and integrate the major points of the course.

■ CONS:

• RSQC2 is a relatively time-consuming activity, especially the first few times it's done.

• It can seem to be or become a waste of time unless everyone participates actively and very effectively. As is true for most of these techniques, if it's overused or used poorly, it can easily become a mindless, pro forma activity.

■ CAVEATS:

• Decide before you use the technique whether you want all, part, or none of the data it generates, and let students know before they start.

• Be prepared for it to go slowly the first one or two times. Make sure to schedule enough time to work through the entire protocol.

- Don't ask students to write down questions or comments about the class unless you are willing to respond to them in some manner.
- Any of the steps in the protocol could take up to 15 minutes. Encourage students to work quickly by announcing and observing time limits.

NOTES

NOTES

EASE-OF-USE RATING: III

■ **DESCRIPTION:**
As noted in the Introduction to this section, students have a tendency to learn what teachers *inspect* rather than what they *expect.* Tests and examinations play a critical role in students' classroom experience. All too often, however, the learning function of testing is overlooked. This simple technique encourages teachers to examine what students think they are learning from the exams and tests, as well as the students' evaluations of how fair, appropriate, useful, and well-constructed the test or exam is.

■ **PURPOSE:**
The overriding purpose of Exam Evaluations is to provide teachers with very specific student reactions to tests and exams so that they can make them more effective as learning and assessment devices.

■ **SUGGESTIONS FOR USE:**
Exam Evaluations can be profitably used to get feedback on any substantial tests or exams, such as weekly, quarterly, or mid-term exams. It's best to administer it while the memory of the test is fresh. One way to do this is to include the Exam Evaluation within the exam itself, as the final section. Another way is to hand out the evaluation very soon after the students have completed the exam.

■ **EXAMPLE:**
An instructor in early childhood development finds writing, giving, and grading tests one of the most difficult and time-consuming parts of teaching. Nonetheless, she is convinced that weekly mini-tests are the most appropriate evaluations for her course and students. She does wonder, however, if it would make any difference to student learning and satisfaction if she switched from short-answer, fill-in tests to multiple-choice tests.

She decides to experiment with the two testing formats to find out. She creates two weekly tests and then translates both into the two formats. She divides the class in half, giving one half the multiple-choice test and the other the short-answer test. The following week, she reverses the groups. After the second week's test, she hands out a short Exam Evaluation sheet containing the following questions:

Exam Evaluation Form (Sample)

In the past two weeks, you have taken two different types of weekly tests—one, multiple-choice and the other, a fill-in, short-answer type. Please answer the following questions about those tests as specifically as possible.

1. Did you feel that one type of test was a fairer assessment of your learning than the other? If so, please explain.
2. Did you enjoy doing one test more than the other? If so, why? (N.B. I particularly want to know whether it was the content or the form that you enjoyed.)

3. Did you learn more from one type of test than from the other? If so, what is it about the test that accounts for that?
4. Which type of test would you prefer to take as your weekly test during the rest of the semester? Why?

■ PROCEDURE:

1. Focus on a type of test or exam that you will or might give more than once during the course. In light of your objectives for the instrument, are there any questions you'd like to ask your students that might help you improve it? If so, write them down.
2. Choose the most important questions, no more than four or five, and decide whether to add them to the test or exam itself or to make up a separate, follow-up evaluation.
3. Whether you incorporate the Exam Evaluation into the test or use it as a follow-up, make sure to schedule the extra time that students will need to respond to the questions.

■ ANALYZING THE DATA YOU COLLECT:

The central focus of the analysis ought to be finding out what students are or aren't learning from the test—a task that requires careful attention to the content of student comments. Try to distinguish comments that address the fairness of *your grading* from those that address the fairness of *the instrument* as a learning assessment. If you've asked students to express their preferences, tabulate those results but link them to the reasons given for those preferences.

■ IDEAS FOR EXTENDING AND ADAPTING:

• Ask students to submit questions they would have included in the test or exam.
• Provide class time for students to compare and discuss their answers in groups. Ask each group to come up with two or three suggestions for improving the test as a learning experience.
• Use the same basic format to assess major course assignments such as papers, problem sets, and homework.

■ PROS:

• Exam Evaluations focus on exams and tests as learning exercises.
• The technique shows respect for students' judgments of their own learning and recognizes their investment in the process.
• It gives teachers feedback on an element of the course that fundamentally affects student learning and satisfaction.

■ CONS:

• The use of this technique may raise questions about tests and exams and grading, that teachers may not want to address.

■ **CAVEATS:**
  • At first, students may find it difficult to determine or express what they have learned from a test. Teachers will probably get better answers if they ask quite specific questions about learning.
  • Don't ask questions about elements of the exam that you aren't willing to consider changing. This is likely to raise student expectations and lead to disappointment.
  • Before you use this technique, consider how you might respond to student objections to the tests—not only how you can defend the tests, but also how you might change them.
  • While you may wish to evaluate a test that won't be given again to the same students—a final exam, for example—the results will not benefit the present students and thus their motivation to respond may be lower.

■ **REFERENCES:**
For a more complete discussion of the use of exams to promote learning, see the McMullen-Pastrick and Gleason (1986) article.

NOTES

NOTES

EASE-OF-USE RATING: IV

■ **DESCRIPTION:**
Quality Control Circles, originally a Japanese management technique for involving teams of workers and managers more directly in industrial planning and problem solving, have been modified and applied to a variety of organizations in the U.S. during the past decade. Impressed by the effectiveness of the Quality Circle approaches used in many U.S. companies and government agencies, a number of instructors have recently experimented with classroom applications of the technique. This assessment technique draws inspiration most directly from the educational adaptations of Quality Control Circles. In this technique, however, the focus is on involving groups of students in structured and ongoing assessment of course materials, activities, and assignments.

■ **PURPOSE:**
Classroom Assessment Quality Circles have two complementary purposes. The first is to provide a vehicle for regularly collecting thoughtful feedback from students on their assessments of readings, exams, activities, and major assignments. The second but no less important purpose is to offer students a structured, positive way to become more actively involved in their classroom learning by becoming better assessors and informants about that experience.

■ **SUGGESTIONS FOR USE:**
Classroom Assessment Quality Circles are a powerful way to reach out and involve students in large lecture courses. It is best suited to flexible courses and instructors. It does not work well, therefore, in courses where the teacher's primary concern is with "covering" a large amount of information during the term.

■ **EXAMPLE:**
Faced with an enrollment of nearly 200 students in his history of Western civilization course, the professor asked for volunteers who would be interested in forming Classroom Assessment Quality Circles to inform and advise him on the course. Thirty students volunteered, but only twenty decided to commit to the Circles after they had discussed it with the professor. He split the twenty volunteers into three more or less even groups and asked each group to meet with him once every three weeks for a scheduled, one-hour long meeting with a clear agenda. After an initial training session with all twenty students, he began meeting with the groups on a rotating basis and saw each group four times in the course of the semester. Each of the twenty Circle members was responsible for contacting, polling or meeting with a group of nine fellow students to elicit their reactions and pass on information from the Quality Circles.

■ **PROCEDURE:**
1. Consider seriously whether or not you want to meet regularly with one or more small groups of students to get their feedback on the course. If you do, decide on the specific elements of the class on which you will focus the Quality Circles' attention and efforts.

2. Ask for volunteers or appoint one or more groups of five to eight students to serve as Classroom Assessment Quality Circles. Make sure to offer the students some compensation for their time and energies. You might grant them credit for one or more assignments or give them a certain number of points toward their final grades for participating.
3. Set up an agenda for the first meeting and give the students a few simple guidelines on how to work effectively in a Quality Circle group. Basically, they must make sure than everyone is heard and that everyone listens actively and constructively—and the instructor must do the same.
4. Make very clear to the members of the Quality Circles which aspects of the course they can expect to affect. Let them also know if there are areas of the course that are not open to discussion.
5. Arrange to meet with the Circles on a regular basis so you have ongoing feedback and they have opportunities to practice their assessment and groupwork skills.
6. Introduce the members of the Classroom Assessment Quality Circles to the rest of the class and encourage class members to seek them out and offer suggestions or criticisms to be discussed at the Circle meetings.

■ IDEAS FOR EXTENDING AND ADAPTING:

• If you have a very large class with several teaching fellows, train them to lead Classroom Assessment Quality Circle groups. The teaching fellows can then form an "inner" Quality Circle to inform and advise you.
• Give the Quality Circles some class time to report to all the students when that seems appropriate.
• Ask members of the Quality Circles to meet together before meetings with you and to draw up proposed agendas for your meetings.

■ PROS:

• Having direct, personal, and purposeful contact with the teacher in a large class can motivate the Circle members to take their participation in the course much more seriously.
• By setting up and cooperating with the Quality Circles, the instructor actively demonstrates his or her commitment to eliciting and listening to student feedback on the course. This clear commitment sends the message to members of the Circles and to the rest of the class that their assessments matter. This encourages students to assess the course more thoughtfully and responsibly.

■ CONS:

• Classroom Assessment Quality Circles take extra time and preparation on the part of teachers and of students. While the students can be compensated with credit toward the grade, it is unlikely that the instructor will be compensated with anything other than the information and satisfaction the technique provides.
• Many of the students who volunteer for the Circles will not have developed the groupwork skills needed to productively use the technique. This means that teachers will have to provide training and guidance in the process itself in order for the Circles to work effectively.

■ **CAVEATS:**
• Perhaps the worst outcome would be for the teacher to start a Quality Circle and then discontinue or lose interest in it. Think hard about the pros and cons before extending the invitation to form the Circles. Think carefully about how you can productively lead the groups, and ask yourself if you are ready to take student suggestions seriously.

■ **REFERENCES AND RESOURCES:**
Useful applications of the Quality Circle technique to college teaching are discussed in Hirshfield (1984), Kogut (1984), and Zeiders and Sivak (1985). The first two articles contain reports on the authors' experiences with the technique.

NOTES

NOTES

BIBLIOGRAPHY

Abrami, P. C. (1985, Spring). Dimension of effective college instruction. *Review of Higher Education, 8*(3), 211-228.

Astin, A. W. (1977). *Four critical years: Effects of college on beliefs, attitudes, and knowledge.* San Francisco: Jossey-Bass.

Astin, A. W. (1985). *Achieving educational excellence.* San Francisco: Jossey-Bass.

Ausubel, D. P. (1968). *Educational psychology: A cognitive view.* New York: Holt, Rinehart & Winston.

Berthoff, A. E. (1982). *Forming/thinking/writing: The composing imagination.* Upper Montclair, NJ: Boynton/Cook.

Blackburn, R. T., & Clark, M. J. (1975, Spring). An assessment of faculty performance: Some correlates between administrator, colleague, student, and self ratings. *Sociology of Education, 48,* 242-256.

Blackburn, R. T., Lawrence, J. H., Ross, S., Okoloko, V. P., Meiland, R., Bieber, J. P., & Street, T. (1986, September). *Faculty as a key resource: A review of the research literature.* Ann Arbor, MI: University of Michigan, National Center for Research to Improve Postsecondary Teaching and Learning.

Bloom, B. S. (Ed). (1956). *Taxonomy of educational objectives: The classification of educational goals. Handbook I: Cognitive domain.* New York: McKay.

Bloom, B. S., Hastings, J. T., & Madaus, G. F. (1971). *Handbook on formative and summative evaluation of student learning.* New York: McGraw-Hill.

Bowen, H. R., with the collaboration of Clecak, P., Doud, J. P., & Douglass, G. K. (1977). *Investment in learning.* San Francisco: Jossey-Bass.

Brown, A. L., Bransford, J. D., Ferrara, R. A., & Campione, J. C. (1983). Learning, remembering, and understanding. In F. H. Flavell & E. M. Markman (Eds.), *Handbook of child psychology Volume III: Cognitive development* (4th ed., pp. 77-166). New York: John Wiley.

Centra, J. A. (1973a). Effectiveness of student feedback in modifying college instruction. *Journal of Educational Psychology, 65*(3), 395-401.

Centra, J. A. (1973b). The student as godfather? The impact of student ratings on academia. *Educational Researcher, 2*(10), 4-8.

Centra, J. A. (1977a, Spring). The how and why of evaluating teaching. *New Directions for Higher Education, 17,* 93-106.

Centra, J. A. (1977b, Winter). Student ratings of instruction and their relationship to student learning. *American Educational Research Journal, 14*(1), 17-24.

Chickering, A. W. (1969). *Education and identity.* San Francisco: Jossey-Bass.

Chipman, S. F., Segal, J. W., & Glaser, R. W. (Eds). (1985). *Thinking and learning skills. Volume 2: Research and open questions.* Hillsdale, NJ: Lawrence Erlbaum.

Cohen, P. A. (1982). Validity of student ratings in psychology courses: A research synthesis. *Teaching of Psychology, 9*(2), 78-82.

Corey, S. M. (1953). *Action research to improve school practices.* New York: Columbia University, Teachers College, Bureau of Publications.

Cranton, P. A., & Smith, R. A. (1986, Spring). A new look at the effect of course characteristics on student ratings of instruction. *American Educational Research Journal, 23*(1), 117-128.

Cross, K. P., & Fideler, E. F. (in press). Assessment in the classroom. *Journal of Higher Education.*

Cunningham, P. M., & Cunningham, J. W. (1987, February). Content area reading-writing lessons. *The Reading Teacher, 40,* 506-512.

Davis, R. (1981, Fall). A plea for the use of student dialogs. *Improving College and University Teaching, 29* (4), 155-161.

Dreher, H. V. (1984, August). Electronic mail: An exemplar of computer use in education. *Educational Technology, 24* (8), 36-38.

Drucker, A. J., & Remmers, H. H. (1950). Do alumni and students differ in their attitude toward instructors? *Purdue University Studies in Higher Education, 70,* 62-74.

Dubin, R., & Taveggia, T. C. (1968). *The teaching-learning paradox: A comparative analysis of college teaching methods.* Eugene, OR: University of Oregon, Center for the Advanced Study of Educational Administration.

Feldman, K. A. (1976). Grades and college students' evaluations of their courses and teachers. *Research in Higher Education, 4,* 69-111.

Feldman, K. A. (1977). Consistency and variability among college students in rating their teachers and courses: A review and analysis. *Research in Higher Education, 6,* 223-274.

Feldman, K. A., & Newcomb, T. M. (1969). *The impact of college on students* (2 vols.). San Francisco: Jossey-Bass.

Gaff, J. G., & Wilson, R. C. (1981, December). The teaching environment. *AAUP Bulletin, 67,* 475-493.

Gleason, M. (1986, February). Getting a perspective on student evaluation. *AAHE Bulletin, 38,* 10-13.

Henry, L. H. (1986). Clustering: Writing (and learning) about economics. *College Teaching, 34* (3), 89-93.

Hirshfield, C. (1984, April 13). The classroom quality circle: A widening role for students. *Innovation Abstracts, 6* (12), 1-2.

Kogut, L. S. (1984, Spring). Quality circles: A Japanese management technique for the classroom. *Improving College and University Teaching, 32* (2), 123-127.

Kohlberg, L. (1971). Stages of moral development as a basis of moral education. In C. M. Beck, B. S. Crittenden, & E. V. Sullivan (Eds.), *Moral education: Interdisciplinary approaches* (pp. 23-92). New York: Newman.

Korn, H. A. (1986, September). *Psychological models explaining the impact of college on students.* Ann Arbor, MI: University of Michigan, National Center for Research to Improve Postsecondary Teaching and Learning.

Krathwohl, D. R., Bloom, B. S., & Masia, B. B. (1964). *Taxonomy of educational objectives: The classification of educational goals. Handbook II: Affective domain.* New York: McKay.

Kulik, J. A., & McKeachie, W. J. (1975). The evaluation of teachers in higher education. In F. N. Kerlinger (Ed.), *Review of research in education* (Vol. 3, pp. 210-240). Itasca, IL: F. E. Peacock.

Loevinger, J., Wessler, R., & Redmore, C. (1970). *Measuring ego development* (2 vols.). San Francisco: Jossey-Bass.

McKeachie, W. J., Pintrich, P. R., Lin, Yi-Guang, & Smith, D. A. F. (1986, September). *Teaching and learning in the college classroom: A review of the research literature.* Ann Arbor, MI: University of Michigan, National Center for Research to Improve Postsecondary Teaching and Learning.

McMullen-Pastrick, M., & Gleason, M. (1986). Examinations: Accentuating the positive. *College Teaching, 34*(4), 135-139.

Mosteller, F. (in press). The "muddiest point in the lecture" as a feedback device. *On Teaching and Learning: The Journal of the Harvard-Danforth Center for Teaching and Learning.*

Novak, J. D., & Gowin, D. B. (1984). *Learning how to learn.* New York: Cambridge University Press.

Pace, C. R. (1979). *Measuring outcomes of college: Fifty years of findings and recommendations for the future.* San Francisco: Jossey-Bass.

Pascarella, E. T. (1985). College environmental influences on learning and cognitive development: A critical review and synthesis. In J. C. Smart (Ed.), *Higher education: Handbook of theory and research* (Vol. 1, pp. 1-61). New York: Agathon Press.

Perry, W. G., Jr. (1970). *Forms of intellectual and ethical development in the college years: A scheme.* New York: Holt, Rinehart & Winston.

Pollio, H. R. (1984, Spring). What students think about and do in college lecture classes. *Teaching-Learning Issues,* (No. 53).

Riegle, R. P., & Rhodes, D. M. (1986). Avoiding mixed metaphors of faculty evaluation. *College Teaching, 34*(4), 123-128.

Roxbury Community College. (1986). *Teaching from strengths conference. May 29-30, 1986.* Boston, MA: Roxbury Community College.

Schon, D. (1986). *Educating the reflective practitioner.* San Francisco: Jossey-Bass.

Segal, J. W., Chipman, S. F., & Glaser, R. (Eds.). (1985) *Thinking and learning skills. Volume 1: Relating instruction to research.* Hillsdale, NJ: Lawrence Erlbaum.

Seldin, P. (1984, April). Faculty evaluation: Surveying policy and practices. *Change, 16*(3), 28-33.

Selfe, C. L., & Arbabi, F. (1986). Writing to learn: Engineering student journals. In A. Young & T. Fulwiler (Eds.), *Writing across the disciplines: Research into practice* (pp. 184-191). Upper Montclair, NJ: Boynton/Cook.

Selfe, C. L., Petersen, B. T., & Nahrgang, C. L. (1986). Journal writing in mathematics. In A. Young & T. Fulwiler (Eds.), *Writing across the disciplines: Research into practice* (pp. 192-207). Upper Montclair, NJ: Boynton/Cook.

Shaughnessy, M. P. (1977). *Errors and expectations: A guide for the teacher of basic writing.* New York: Oxford University Press.

Skeff, K. M. (1983, September). Evaluation of a method for improving the teaching performance of attending physicians. *The American Journal of Medicine, 75,* 465-470.

Student Learning Outcomes Subcommittee. (1987). *Fifth progress report.* Trenton, NJ: New Jersey State Department of Higher Education, New Jersey College Outcomes Evaluation Program (COEP).

Study Group on the Conditions of Excellence in American Higher Education. (1984). *Involvement in learning*. Washington, DC: National Institute of Education.

Weaver, R. L., & Cotrell, H. W. (1985, Fall/Winter). Mental aerobics: The half-sheet response. *Innovative Higher Education, 10,* 23-31.

Weinstein, C., & Mayer, R. (1986). The teaching of learning strategies. In M. C. Wittrock (Ed.), *Handbook of research on teaching* (pp. 315-327). New York: Macmillan.

Willingham, W. W. with the assistance of Young, J. W., & Morris, M. M. (1985). *Success in college: The role of personal qualities and academic abilities.* New York: College Entrance Examination Board.

Wilson, R. C. (1986, March/April). Improving faculty teaching: Effective use of student evaluations and consultants. *Journal of Higher Education, 57*(2), 196-211.

Wilson, R. C., & Gaff, J. G., with Dienst, E. R., Wood, L., & Bavry, J. L. (1975). *College professors and their impact on students.* New York: Wiley.

Wilson, W. (1925). The spirit of learning. (1909). In *Selected literary and political papers and addresses of Woodrow Wilson* (Vol. 1, pp. 244-265). New York: Grosset & Dunlap.

Young, A., & Fulwiler, T. (Eds.). (1986). *Writing across the disciplines: Research into practice.* Upper Montclair, NJ: Boynton/Cook.

Zeiders, B. B., & Sivak, M. (1985, November). Quality circles from A to Z: King Arthur to Theory Z. *The Clearing House, 59*(4), 123-124.